# naked in the woods

T0170482

# naked in the woods

MY UNEXPECTED YEARS IN A HIPPIE COMMUNE

MARGARET GRUNDSTEIN

Oregon State University Press | Corvallis

The paper in this book meets the guidelines for permanence and durability of the Committee on Production Guidelines for Book Longevity of the Council on Library Resources and the minimum requirements of the American National Standard for Permanence of Paper for Printed Library Materials Z39.48-1984.

**Library of Congress Cataloging-in-Publication Data**
Grundstein, Margaret.
  Naked in the woods : my unexpected years in a hippie commune / Margaret Grundstein.
    pages cm
  ISBN 978-0-87071-807-6 (paperback) — ISBN 978-0-87071-808-3 (e-book)
1. Grundstein, Margaret. 2. Hippies—United States—Biography. 3. Communal living—Oregon—Biography. 4. Country life—Oregon—Anecdotes. 5. Women—United States—Biography. 6. Hippies—Oregon—Social life and customs—20th century. 7. Hippies—Social conditions—20th century—Anecdotes. 8. Poverty—United States—Psychological aspects. 9. Baby boom generation—United States—Biography. 10. Young adults—United States—Attitudes—20th century. 11. United States—Social conditions—1960-1980—Anecdotes. 12. Oregon—Biography. I. Title. II. Title: My unexpected years in a hippie commune.
HQ799.7.G78 2015
307.77'409795—dc23

                    2015006811

© 2015 Margaret Grundstein
All rights reserved. First published in 2015 by Oregon State University Press
Printed in the United States of America

**Oregon State University Press**
121 The Valley Library
Corvallis OR 97331-4501
541-737-3166 • fax 541-737-3170
www.osupress.oregonstate.edu

*This book is dedicated to my daughters . . . the beat goes on.*

## Preface

Memory is elusive. To conjure this book I slid down the rabbit hole of my past following the imperative "write me." Large fragments of time calved off my daily life, to be spent in the alternate universe of my memory. My body, meanwhile, continued to thrive in the parallel present. While writing, I rummaged down deep, trying to re-live and re-feel what I experienced forty years ago. There are events I could fact check and experiences that could only be tested by the veracity of feelings within me. If any errors exist, it is because memory truly is elusive, to say nothing of subjective. This is my story, set in an historic time, a tale to be told. Any errors are mine, although I couldn't find them.

I have fictionalized the names of the individuals who are identified in the book as Adi, Brandi, Daisy, Flow, Gilang, Hakim, Hamdan, James, Jean, Kathy, Kit, Laura, Lev, Lorene, Martine, Ozzie, and Ruth. Although these names are fictional, the narrative is factual. Any similarity between these fictional names and the names of any real people is strictly coincidental.

## Acknowledgments

My first thank you is to the Oregon State University Press. They have, and continue to be, both supportive and gracious. I am very pleased and proud that *Naked in the Woods* has found a home with them. But in the beginning there was the manuscript. To bring it to completion I worked with many people. First and foremost was Jan Cherubin, my editor. We met midway through the work. Jan offered sensitive insight and constructive discussion that sent me back to my computer again and again, refining story and concepts until the book felt done. Other readers were also generous with their time and helpful with their comments. These include Abby Child, a strong artist and lifelong friend who offered intelligence, artistic sensibility, and support. I also would like to thank Barbara Einstein, who unknowlingly started me on this journey, as well as Dana Liston, Anna Boorstin, Ann Bronston, Gene Stein, Arleen Torres, Diane Caughey, Judy Hammond, Lynn Eisenberg, Nicole Haimes, Albee Gordon, Yardenna Hurvitz, my sister Miriam Levin, and my daughters Morgan and Mckay, along with their spouses, Jesse and Nico. In addition I am grateful to Carol Schlanger. Our dialogues helped me launch *Naked in the Woods* from my original concept to a completed book and our debates helped me give it form.

Once a book is completed, it needs to be launched. Kim Dower has been dedicated, available, gracious and supportive in her efforts to bring *Naked in the Woods* to a larger audience. I am impressed and thankful.

My original conception of *Naked in the Woods* was a communal telling of a communal tale. This Rashomon effect did not prove practical, but I did interview and/or receive brief written summaries from many of the main participants. Thank you to Roggie, Clint, Kokia, Paul, Katrina, Lenny, Steve, and Guy.

I would also like to thank Hakim, my first husband. Although our personal relationship had some significant bumps, I will always be grateful to him for leading me forward into the wonderful journey of *Naked in the Woods*. Without him I would not have found my way past my caution into the adventure that broadened my mind, coloring who I was for the rest of my life.

And finally before the music swells and the handsome gigolos appear who will usher me off the stage, I would like to thank my father, who modeled for me that the life of the mind is what keeps us vital and that we are never too old to start something new.

Thank you, thank you, thank you, to each and every one of you.

# Contents

# Prologue

IN 1969, I WAS PART OF A GROUP OF RADICALS at Yale University trying to create a community where we could live in peace and innocence. Change seemed possible. San Francisco celebrated the Summer of Love, Martin Luther King Jr. taught us the power of nonviolence, and Woodstock was iconic before the mud in Max Yasger's fields had dried. Then armored tanks rolled across the campus.

We advocated peace, ignoring the implications of our growing militancy as students occupied campus buildings, organized strikes, and demanded an end to the war in Vietnam and racism at home. Nationally, the civil rights movement shifted with the arrival of thirty Black Panthers at the California State Assembly flaunting rifles and shotguns to protest arms-control legislation. The country, watching on television, shuddered and looked to the locks on their doors and windows. Cities burned, assassins murdered Malcolm X and the Reverend King, and the National Guard, dressed like invading aliens in gas masks and goggles, killed four students at Kent State, injuring nine. This was revolution.

Swaying together singing "We Shall Overcome" was no longer enough. The tanks lumbering through my neighborhood, clanking down my street brought home the futility of confrontational tactics. We needed a new plan, one that was plausible and released us from the politics of mutual hate. If we couldn't change the world, we would change ourselves and build communities, where, as the Beatles told us, "All You Need is Love." In Vermont, New Mexico, Virginia, and Oregon—any place where land was available and people sparse—students dropped out, looking for a more peaceful revolution. The back-to-the-land movement showed us a way we could love ourselves, each other, and the dirt that fed us.

After graduation, my new husband and I, along with ten of our friends, headed west like generations before us. Our covered wagon was a Chevy van. We abandoned indoor plumbing, electricity, supermarkets, and the benefits of our graduate Ivy League degrees for one-hundred-and-sixty acres in the backwoods of the Pacific Northwest, seeking the sweetness of childhood without sacrificing adult perks. "Freaks," they called us, not far off the mark. We, in turn, felt anointed by God; that is, if God is love. Our adventure lasted five years, our quest timeless, with ripples that lap on the shoreline of the present. The future grows out of the past.

Young families in Detroit, Los Angeles, and the White House are now harvesting dinner from their organic gardens. Portland has over ten organizations to promote poultry-raising at home, including one that offers a tour of twenty-two coops and a chance to meet the chickens. The longing to connect is immutable, even as teenagers text and adults boast of six hundred Facebook friends. We yearn to be in touch with the land, ourselves, and each other, seeking transcendence even as we balance on our feet of clay.

I wore my hippie status proudly, even defiantly. We had been raised to be good, to share, to see beyond race and income, and to make the world a better place. Every childhood story, parental exhortation, and moral parable set the mold; virtue and the search for it brought meaning to life. I was willing to risk everything for a chance to live from my better self, to experience the peace of love without sacrificing the thrill of adventure. My parents thought I achieved the good life with my entry into Yale. They were wrong. I found it naked in the woods.

What we didn't know was that *utopia*, in its Greek roots, meant nowhere. Money was a problem. We refused to earn any. "Steal this book," Abbie Hoffman exhorted in his 1971 work of the same name, a do-it-yourself manual for revolution against the Pig Empire. To his embarrassment, the book sold over a quarter of a million copies, ending up on the bestseller list of the *New York Times*. That was the conundrum. Rip off the Man, or be the Man? We chose the former, living on unemployment insurance and food stamps, beneficiaries of Lyndon Johnson's Great Society, augmenting government largesse by gleaning from the abundance around us: catch a salmon, pick some berries, harvest the wild greens. Our lives were rich. Sharing was easy in the beginning. Lean times proved more difficult.

Living together was a challenge. Barely adept as couples, we were now joined as family: eating, bathing, working, birthing, and dreaming together. "Love one another" is a great concept until you try it, especially in tight quarters with no exit from annoying habits or characters flaws. We were all iconoclasts with strong egos, used to setting paths, not following them. Men struggled with dominance, their alpha-dog genetics in conflict with our new communal ethic. For women, it was the opposite. We had thrown away our bras and embraced our strength. Now we were shackled again, feminists dependent on the strong bodies and wilderness skills of our men.

Then we met our ultimate nemesis: land ownership. We thought we had left old values behind, ignoring our cultural DNA, but one-hundred-and-sixty acres of forested mountainside was hard capital, representing past labor and future gain. Who would own it: all of us, or one of us? Rifts formed. Eden was beyond our reach. We were human, after all.

Did we fail? The measure is not the duration of our community, but to what degree we rode the rapids of the pent-up need for change in western, middle-class lives. In that sense, we surely succeeded. We were children of our times, going "further," just like the name emblazoned on the front of Ken Kesey and the Merry Pranksters' bus. "Is That All There Is?" Peggy Lee sang in the late sixties, a lament to the existential bleakness of every-day life. No! There *must* be more! We took a leap of faith and dropped out, taking cues from idealists before us, the world we left behind, irrelevant.

Our struggle to belong, to each other and the earth, was more influ-ential than we had anticipated. It is easy to dismiss hippies as carica-tures: peace and love, flowers in our hair, got a joint? But we were part of something bigger, a time when people burst free, shucking off old skins to emerge fresh and hopeful. Over time, history defines context. The present demands action. Today becomes tomorrow. Forty years later I see our vi-sion embedded in every preschool garden, organic produce shelf, herbal cure, and restaurant community table.

We lived an adventure, changed ourselves, and left our legacy. The eve-ning news covers a black president in the oval office instead of sits-ins at the Woolworth's lunch counter. Women run multinational corpora-tions and are on the cusp of running our country. Sexual freedom, gender identity, gay marriage, environmentalism, alternative health care, and the politics of food are part of the national dialogue. Organic is big business. Weed is medicinal.

Now it is time to add our tale to the collective consciousness, to feed the dreams for those who follow. My hope, like any storyteller, is to en-tertain and transport you while passing on the stories of our tribe. Sit with me around a fire in the Aboriginal bush, the Amazon rainforest of the Kayapo, the Great Plains of the Sioux, or better yet, our communal kitchen in Floras Creek, Oregon. The flickering light reflects off our faces. Outside our circle is darkness. We have come together. My mouth is open, my hands raised high as I work to bring you along with me. Feel the words rise like sparks from the fire up to the Dreamtime of every good tale. If you are lucky, you will become a part of something larger. I know I did.

# PART I

## New Haven

# CHAPTER 1  Here Comes the Sun

I WAS QUITE PLEASED WITH MYSELF AS I STOOD in front of the Art and Architecture Building at Yale, my new academic home. It was 1968. Before entering, I took a moment to smooth my shirtwaist dress and adjust the straw bag neatly hanging from my shoulder. Behind me a noise rumbled. A bus, swirling with color, pulled up to the curb, paisley bedspreads billowing from its dusty windows. With a hiss, the door opened and out gamboled a ragtag band, a tribe of hippies, wild hair flying, bare feet dancing. The Hog Farm was on the road. I watched, fascinated, as they threw tattered suitcases from the bus and shoved cardboard boxes out the windows.

"Anything I can do to help?" I tentatively asked a young woman about my age, shifting my purse higher up on my shoulder.

She was barefoot, in bell bottoms and a gauzy top, feathers dangling from the ends of the macramé cord around her waist.

"Sure," she said. "You can give me a hand with some of this stuff. Just be careful," she blithely warned in passing. "We've got scabies."

I moved on, but the Hog Farmers had left their mark, one that would alter the course of my life.

For me, achievement was a given, academic or professional, it didn't matter. Just be smart, analytic, and comfortably compensated. My dad, a public administration professor, pushed for the legal profession. "It encompasses all of life," he argued, trying to persuade a burnt-out high school senior to follow his dream. He was ahead of his time. In 1961, educated women aspired to become teachers, nurses, and administrative assistants. None of it seemed like much of a prize at the end of the rainbow of youth. Instead, I set my eye on a graduate degree in urban planning at Yale. They accepted me into the master's program for fall of 1968, a year before allowing women to matriculate in the undergraduate colleges.

I arrived in New Haven with a clear picture of my future: After long days spent fighting to renew America's cities with reason and taste, I would retreat with my lawyer husband into our large colonial home where our two children, glowing accessories in the grand scheme, co-existed alongside fluted soufflé dishes and framed Marimekko prints, all from Design Research, the Mecca of my domestic dreams. Instead I met the Hog Farm, the *amuse bouche* for what was to come.

Within weeks, another harbinger appeared. Members of the Living Theatre, thin and wraith-like, slouched past the Art and Architecture Building in a slow parade of haunted suffering, headed toward the school of drama. I went to their first performance alone, buying one of the last tickets.

"Take the leap. Trust. You are at the precipice," they cried, exhorting us to fall backwards off the proscenium into their waiting arms below. "I'll do it," the guy two seats over from me volunteered, on his feet and running to the stage. "I won't," I thought, hunkering down, not wanting to be noticed, as actors with skin colors that defied race roamed through the seated audience.

Two nights later I was back like a moth to light, once again titillated and aghast, a familiar fulcrum for me. Midway through Paradise Now, troupe members started to disrobe as they recited a litany of repression. "I am not allowed to travel without a passport," one called out behind me. To my left, slipping out of his pants, another actor announced, "I cannot travel freely." On stage an actress pulled her blouse over her head. "The body itself, that of which we are made, is taboo," she cried. "The culture represses love. I am outside the gates of paradise."

I tried to watch without looking as they paraded naked, strutting and weaving through boundaries that moments ago had seemed set in stone. They were comfortable. I was not, instinctively averting my eyes, embarrassed to be caught seeing them. The actors called for all of us to join them in a dance out of the theatre and into the street. All around me people stood up, the audience diminishing as the snaking line of chanters grew. Which was worse, joining in and feeling manipulated or watching them go by, one of the few uptight jerks left sitting in the theatre, damned by my own skepticism? I jumped up, chanting and hollering in moderation, taking the leap but not quite knowing how to let go.

By winter, the season inside me had also changed. Timothy Leary spoke in the same neo-gothic hall where I had dutifully transcribed lectures on the history of architecture a few days earlier. Leary was tall and elegantly thin, surrounded by an entourage of men that faded to the background as he stepped forward on the raised podium, quieting the overflowing room. He wore a honey-colored suede jacket with foot-long fringe hanging off the arms. Every time he gestured, the fringe on his coat moved with him, an erotic chorus of leather that draped and swayed in backup to his voice. I was entranced. There was nothing intellectual about it, just the call of sensuality and freedom. Inside me a voice spoke. "I need that jacket."

Within me and around me change was the verb, spontaneously erupting both culturally and politically. Freedom Riders rode south to fight Jim Crow laws. Three hundred thousand demonstrators marched on Washington demanding an end to racism. The Klu Klux Klan murdered activists trying to register black voters. Inner cities erupted. Radicals, liberals, black nationalists, hippies, professors, women's groups, and war veterans surrounded the Pentagon. In Chicago demonstrators and police battled outside the Democratic National Convention. Women struck for equality at home and at work. Columbia students mobilized against racism and Vietnam, holding three administrators hostage. Berkeley staked its place with the Free Speech Movement. In Paris, students and workers took to the barricades. I was nothing if not a competitive achiever in this battle for justice. No need to take a bus to Mississippi, I could be a freedom fighter in my own backyard. We made our move, confronting the school of architecture, demanding the acceptance of more minority students into the city planning department. What a shift. Last fall I was preening over the upward turn of my future. And now, what's this? Thumbing my nose at the very institution whose stamp of approval I wore with pride.

"The time has come!" I called out. "Yes, it has arrived, pulled right into the station!" High on adrenaline, my inhibitions dropped away. I stood behind the makeshift podium in the soaring three-story amphitheatre of the Art and Architecture Building and made my debut speech, La Pasionaria in a miniskirt and high heels, lots of leg and plenty of attitude.

Over two hundred painters, architects, and planners gathered before me, many of them friends and familiar faces. Faculty and staff watched from the balconies that surrounded the space, high above the fray. Two professors, my mentors, leaned over the railing peering intently. I nodded. Separate from them, another professor, newly appointed, stood alone, his face aghast as he watched his future crumble. Secretaries clustered outside the second-story dean's office. Administrators were nowhere in sight.

"This school, our home, is not in order. We have work to do, not somewhere else, but here, here in our own backyard." I gestured to the space around us.

"Piles of privileged racism have been swept under the rug. We stand here complicit." I was on a roll, the words pouring out of my mouth, possessed by my communion with virtue and thrill. "Are we going to let bigotry prevail or will we demand, yes demand, that our voice for equality be heard? Asking is over. Now is the time for action." And it was. On Yale letterhead I informed, with pleasure, one Mr. Herring, an African American applicant, of his acceptance into our program. The missive was signed, "Margaret Grundstein for the City Planning Forum," our new ad hoc governing body. Seven days later, the same Mr. Herring received correspondence from the school of architecture, also on official letterhead. It informed him, with regret, of his lack of admittance. This letter was signed Howard S. Weaver, Dean. One skirmish lost, onto the next.

These were the years when I expected to meet my future spouse, a solid, left-leaning professional, the perfect match for my ambition. One man caught my eye, Ken, the most outrageous designer in the school as well as the charismatic center of South Coast, an offshoot of the radical Ant Farm architectural collective. Ken was a pied piper, seducing through design and drugs. Inflatable buildings were his medium, psychedelics his muse. When he invited me to the Beaux Arts Ball I felt anointed, the princess of youth, vision, and prestige. Yet all Ken brought and all he represented were still grounded in architectural tradition, given legitimacy by their presence at Yale. Success was always in our sights, even as we flirted with the edges.

The afternoon of the ball we met at Ken's house to work on costumes. He led me to the kitchen where two empty tuna cans lay strewn on the Formica tabletop. Inspired, Ken cleaned them out and used a church key to punch triangular holes on opposite sides of each tin. While I watched, puzzled, he found some twine and tied the cans together, fashioning a bikini top for me. Then he dug through a pile of Texas flags, Mylar sheets, and gas station tinsel to discover pieces of silvery fabric, that, when knotted together, formed a bikini bottom. I was confused. Where was this heading?

Ken let me know. His plan was to transform us into space aliens by smearing green paint all over our bodies, ignoring the fact that the ball had a fifties theme. I could wear the tuna cans but he would be naked. Fine for him, I thought, but I had fantasies of glamour. Looking like seaweed would detract from my sex appeal. I refused. Ken, undeterred, stained his face, hair, body, and genitalia the color of algae and draped parachutes over his nakedness and my tin cans. Then he dropped a tab of acid.

We arrived like royalty from another consciousness. Stopping for a moment at the threshold to the party, I pulled back my parachute, letting it fan behind me from my shoulders like a regal train, my head held high in the central opening. Now I was ready. We entered together, side by side, making waves as we moved through the crowd. Ken gradually drifted off into an acid reality. I, high on myself and the music, danced all night, lowering my parachute only when the strings between my tuna cans frayed and broke. How could life get better than this?

Then I met Hakim. A mutual friend introduced us in the café of the Art and Architecture Building. I was singularly unimpressed. He was a short Asian guy in a dark blue blazer, khaki pants, and penny loafers, high contrast to the outré art students. "Boring" was my take.

A few months later we ran into each other again. Gone was the preppy New Englander from Jakarta. In his place, wearing a leather trench coat, aviator shades, and ankle boots, was a hip black activist sporting attitude as well as a girlfriend. Hak was with Lorene, also wearing sunglasses, and together they cut quite a couple. She was slender and elegant, with café au lait skin, and close to a head taller than Hakim. Her crowning glory was a stunning Afro that added extra inches to her height and a lot of moxie to her presence. That hair shot thunderbolts of racial confrontation and feminist sexuality. I got the message. My curls were not yet free, and I had to swallow to keep from choking on my white guilt, but woman to woman the challenge came through, loud and clear. We needed to stand up and be counted. Our day had come.

Lorene's hair went up and out. Hak's hung heavy, straight, and dark, sensually tucked into the upturned collar of his open coat. He was small but powerfully built. I could not help but notice that this was a new man standing in front of me, that whiff of danger quite the perfume.

Hak, I learned, had dropped out of Yale graduate school to become an organizer in The Hill, the black neighborhood in New Haven. Being Indonesian had its advantages. Racially Hak could morph in almost any direction. I took the news in stride. We were all becoming activists one way or another.

A few months later the calls began. At the time I did not realize that Hakim had a girlfriend to fit each persona. While studying economics at

Harvard, he dated Muffy, a mainliner from Philadelphia, the perfect foil for his presumed path as CEO of a large corporation. As he tried to bridge the divide between radical black organizer and white political activist, I was next.

"Hey, Margaret. It's Hak. How about getting together?"

Even with his new outlaw persona, I wasn't interested. "I can't. I'm in the middle of cutting out a dress," I replied. Living on a student budget, I made most of my own clothes, a skill I learned from my mother.

Meanwhile, Hak's phone calls kept coming, as did my refusals. Ever the strategist, Hakim upped the ante. "Hey," he announced, the phone interrupting me as my sewing machine was rounding the last buttonhole on a mini-dress. "You inspired me, so now I'm sewing a jacket for myself. I need help with the sleeves. Can you give me a hand?" Silence on my end. *He's* sewing a jacket? That's what *I* did. *His* jackets came from J. Press. Sleeves were tricky. They took more than rudimentary skill. Who was this man who would take on a woman's work to get through the door?

"Margaret, are you still there?"

"Yes," I answered, my voice less certain than before. How was I supposed to get out of this? I pulled myself together and asked the obvious, "When did you start sewing?"

"Just a few weeks ago," he said. "I asked my neighbor to teach me, but I'm stuck on the sleeves."

I was stuck too. I didn't know how to tell him no. "Sure," I offered, trying to fake a welcoming tone. "Come on over and I'll see what we can do." In half an hour Hak and I, on our hands and knees, were fitting fabric into the armholes of his partially completed jacket. Working together was fun. I had never sewn with a man before. Hak jumped in like he did with everything, eager and confident. His enthusiasm charmed me. I relaxed and started to open up.

Hakim was unlike anyone I had met before. It wasn't so much that he was Indonesian. That should have been familiar territory for me. My father, affectionately known as Grundy, taught public administration at Wayne State in Detroit. Our home was often full of foreign students, usually middle-aged public servants furthering their careers. These were family affairs where my parents, siblings, and I shared ourselves with visitors who missed their own wives and children. My mother, who cooked, was respectfully honored for her contribution as she basked in the reflected light from her spouse.

One semester, when I was nine, three Indonesian students joined us for dinner. Among them was Mr. Sukarno, whose angular brown face reflected his wiry body. He was about forty and wore a white, short-sleeved shirt and dark trousers, his collar tropically open at the neck. After the main meal, we gathered in the living room where Mr. Sukarno prepared to perform a traditional Indonesian dance, his now bare feet planted side by side on the Oriental rug in front of our fireplace. My family and I were the audience, along with the other Indonesian students. They too were dressed in dark slacks and white, short sleeved shirts. My pregnant mother sat in the overstuffed chair closest to the dining room, my younger brother Leon tucked in close beside her. Miriam, my older sister, picked a big chair for herself and I sat on the couch, flanked by Mr. Sukarno's cohorts. All of us, except for my father, leaned forward expectantly. He stood alone, resting against the wall; part of us but a bit separate, alert as the host, holding his pipe in his hand and his tenement past in the recesses of his mind, a childhood far from this evening.

The room was silent. Mr. Sukarno faced forward, his eyes closed, his attention inward. We waited. Abruptly, he opened his eyes wide and made loud clicking noises with the back of his tongue, his jaw rigid. Against this sound Mr. Sukarno sharply pulled his left leg up like a marionette, forming a right angle at his knee. His foot remained parallel to our floor, accenting the stylized form. I watched, embarrassed, for him and for me. Nobody did this in living rooms. He was so earnest. How could he make himself so vulnerable? The performance continued for ten minutes, no accompaniment except for the metronome like clicking from the back of Mr. Sukarno's jaw, his face impassive as he performed ancient ritualized movements that told stories I didn't know.

After the dance, and many appreciative comments, my mother set out dessert: Velvet Crumb cake, a specialty of hers, right off the Bisquick box. My father put Frank Sinatra on the stereo to revive the conviviality of the evening. I waited, slow to find my place. Everyone headed toward the dining room except Mr. Sukarno, who, moving in the opposite direction, joined me where I sat alone on the couch. His attention made me uncomfortable. I wanted to be ignored, not noticed. What could I say to this man who had just stood in front of our fireplace making bodily noises and disjointed movements? Mr. Sukarno solved the problem. He opened the conversation with the same intensity he brought to his dance. "Do you think," he asked me, "that Frank Sinatra really believes the words he is singing?" I was nine. The thought had never occurred to me. People sang and you listened. I felt cornered. My eyes slid past Mr. Sukarno toward the cake. Broiled coconut topping was my favorite.

Now things were different. This was my apartment and my couch. Hakim sat there, smart, confident, a man who liked risk. He was equally comfortable hanging out with young Italian toughs from the local pool hall, smoking dope with the grassroots leaders of the black community, or hosting his old roommate from Harvard, whose family had a private foundation for distributing largesse.

Blissfully unaware, I stepped into my future. Hakim courted me so forcefully I felt I neither had, nor wanted, a choice in the matter. I was hungry for what he offered. The more I opened, the bigger he became in my life, so much so that ultimately even my three inches over his height seemed to disappear. We moved in together at the end of my first year in New Haven, the summer of 1969.

We were a couple, stepping high and feeling good. Hak had money in his pocket and liked spending it, an enjoyable contrast for me. Dinner? Hop in the BMW, New York is two hours down the road. Janis Joplin? Hak has tickets. Diana Ross? Central Park, here we come. Hak loved having a good time. My life expanded. I needed Hak to break down my walls and open me up. And he loved me. Why would he fight so hard for me if he didn't? I felt safe in that knowledge.

The times had changed and, like the rest of my generation, I thought I was ready. The fifties were over. James Brown, the King of Soul, was right: "Papa's Got a Brand New Bag." America's cities rioted, women burned their bras outside the Miss America Pageant, vets and draft dodgers protested Vietnam, pouring dirty secrets out into the streets. Money flowed and drugs lost their taboo, mind-expanding psychedelics as well as the hard stuff. Abby Hoffman threw dollar bills from the gallery of the New York Stock Exchange. Pranksters invaded politics. Never trust anyone over thirty. Music was everywhere: raw, sexy funk, the Beatle's exhortation that "All You Need is Love," Woodstock as a nation. Like Clark Kent, we stepped out of our suits, but publicly, no need for secrets any longer. This was *our* time. Hakim held out his hand and I grabbed on, ready to be pulled into the oxygenated air where he swooped and soared, often gleefully executing rolls just for the fun of it.

Drugs were definitely a part of the package. Have a toke. Snort a line. Not enough? Try a tab. Acid, mind-expanding and God-inducing, was the newest gift to consciousness. But I knew myself. Drugs were not for me. I couldn't even tolerate alcohol. One drink at dinner and I was hung over by dessert. All the hard-sell advertising was fine, but I read the disclaimers, the fine print of suicides and young minds gone berserk under the influence of this holy sacrament. I held myself tightly. Drugs were dangerous. They could burst a hole, breaching the dike. At the same time, behind my fortifications, I longed to break free, fearful of the deluge but tired of the wall. Politics was intellectual and moral. That I could understand. Mind-altering substances were another matter.

October of my second year I ran into Ken on campus. He was mildly tripping on acid. I wouldn't have known if he hadn't told me, his slightly distracted air belying anything more powerful than a strong joint.

"Come join me," he invited.

"You know I'm not good with drugs," I protested.

"But this is gentle, very pure."

"What if it isn't gentle for me?" I parried, but not with much force.

"Don't worry," he soothed, the mantra of every pied piper.

I listened, seduced by his music.

Ken led me back to his house through the sunlight of an early autumn afternoon.

I had been living with Hakim for four months and knew I needed to call him. He was not going to be happy. Taking acid with Ken was tantamount to having an affair. I was accepting another man as my guide and guru, sharing something intimate, a fact I realized but didn't want to think about. Ken was a pro; his experience reassured me. If I was going to take LSD it would be with Ken. Hakim had never done acid and I couldn't trust him to protect me. He always pushed, needing what *he* wanted. This trip was mine. Ken would carry me through.

Reluctantly but responsibly, I called. "I'm with Ken," I told Hakim. "We dropped some acid." His response shocked me. "What? You want me to come home? Hak, I can't. The acid's going to kick in." Hak persisted. I listened, filling up with his need until it became mine. "Okay, let me tell Ken. I'll be there soon."

Of course I agreed. How could I tell Hak I didn't trust him, that he was too forceful, too strong over me? And how could I ignore that I was betraying Hak? We were living together. This was for him, not Ken.

I asked Ken to walk me home. The acid was smooth but I could feel its power. Everything teetered on morphing out of its true self into a more intensified reality. I didn't hallucinate but I could feel the force of the drug. Once would be enough.

At home, Hakim sat with me and let me have my trip, supportive without any demands. He did, however, have plans. Acid sounded great to him, particularly screwing together while our synapses fired away unimpeded. He had an agenda and needed me on board, a point made clear when he came home a few weeks later, smiling from ear to ear, waving a small packet.

"Guess what? I've got something for us."

He looked so happy. I gave him a big hug. "What did you get?" I asked, playing my part in his surprise.

"Two tabs," he replied, holding out the folded paper, quite pleased with himself.

Bam. There went the mood. I was incredulous. "What are you thinking? I'm not going to do acid again."

"You were willing to take it with Ken. I want you to try it with me."

I could feel myself slip into the defensive, always the weaker position. "Hak, please don't."

"Just once, you and me. The sex will be great."

"It's too scary. I don't want to take it again."

"Don't worry," he tried to reassure me. "I took care of everything." Hak opened the drawer to his desk where there were four capsules of Thorazine, a powerful anti-psychotic sold on the street as an antidote to a bad trip. "See," he said. "All it takes is one to bring you down." Hak smiled at me. "I promise, there's nothing to worry about."

I thought I owed this to Hakim, but why couldn't he respect my reluctance? Hak always pressed his foot on the gas and crashed through my barricades, which, in truth, were usually flimsy. Fighting was rare in my family. We recoiled from the heat of arguments as soon as the emotional kindling began to smoke. Retreat! Back off! That is what we knew. Big rifts could form. Love can't hold this. As children, we learned our lessons well, not understanding that the love bought by appeasement wasn't as strong as that tempered in a well-managed burn.

"Okay," I sighed, attuned to the call of his need over mine, "but this is it. I am never taking LSD again."

The acid was laced with speed. If there was one thing I did not need, it was the added effect of uppers. My brain naturally fired at an accelerated rate. The tab kicked in strong and never stopped. All my fear and resentment shook loose, each liberated synapse feeding on the next.

"I can't do this," I whimpered, helpless in the dark space of drug-enhanced dread. "Get me out," I pleaded in terror.

"Just lie down," Hak encouraged, patting some blankets on the floor, trying to soothe me and get into my pants. The only thing I wanted was to get out of my brain. There was no oneness with God or transcendental truth for me. No, all I had was fear, a sucking black hole. I was going mad.

"I need those pills, Hak. Where are they?"

"Just relax. Everything will be good."

"Please, please, please. I can't do this."

Finally, Hak got it. This trip was *over*. He fumbled with the desk drawer for the stash of Thorazine, I took one. He took one.

"It's not working!" I screamed. "Get me out of here!"

Hak took a second Thorazine and called his friend Alex from the Hill to drive us to the hospital. By the time we got to the emergency room I started to feel better; the downer had kicked in and my fear had abated. After all, here were people in crisp, white uniforms who could help. I walked up to the reception desk and leaned on the counter. Behind me were Alex and Hak. I took the lead. This time I was in charge. It was embarrassing to tell these responsible people what we had done, but that was a minor snag on the way to salvation.

"He took two Thorazines so that he could help me because I was having a bad trip." I informed the nurse. "I only took one."

"He took two?" was their incredulous exclamation. They whisked Hakim away, tending to his potential overdose while I sat out in the hallway with Alex. I didn't care. In fact I was happy. Finally, I relaxed into the tail end of the tempered acid trip and enjoyed animated bubble men that inflated and dissolved, joyously smiling at me through the examination room door. They were white, just like the hospital, and full of good cheer; happy, energetic cartoons in the style of Peter Max whose graphics defined the times.

Two weeks later in the lobby of the gas company, awaiting my turn to pay our utility bill, I noticed the brick wall at the back of the room start to slump at one corner and then crumble into a heap on the floor. The crash happened silently, a soundless disintegration that left a gaping, black hole. No one seemed to notice but me. Everyone else continued to stand in line, attentive to their slow march toward the front counter. Something had cracked, and it wasn't just the wall. My mind had given way. I needed to get home.

I stepped out of line and headed back to the security of our apartment. There I crawled into bed and called Hak. But it was no good. No place was safe. Clutching the covers, I shook and quivered. Hakim came home and tried to comfort me as I rocked back and forth crying. Finally, he drove me to student health services where they gave me an injection that knocked me out. When I came to, they started me on anti-psychotics, Stelazine this time, along with talk therapy. After a day I was discharged, but chose to stay with friends, Howie and Eadie, instead of returning home. Their apartment seemed normal with neutral colors and a stable couple who could cushion me in their care, not asking anything but giving everything. In contrast, at home I had painted two of our living room walls glossy red and Hakim was waiting for me, always pulling at me even as he gave to me.

While I recuperated from my bad trip, I let Hak visit me at Howie and Eadie's. He stayed longer each time. I liked seeing him, but the thought of being alone with Hak in our shiny crimson apartment made me turn my head away. He repainted our walls in an effort to lure me back, but everything was moving too fast, slipping and sliding between unpredictable coordinates. Maybe Alice could tolerate the free fall through the rabbit hole, but I was not up to it. Where did I get off usurping the power of the dean of my graduate program? Now my fortifications had been breached. Acid broke my synapses loose, my mind psychotically creating its own reality. And then there was Hakim. I had lowered the door across my moat and now he was king, running my show at a faster, more radical pace than I could handle. Women, even strong women, still fell hard, losing power in the unspoken contracts of intimacy. My center was gone and I had imploded. On whom could I depend? I had stepped further than I wanted and was unmoored, holding on to Hakim, my strength and my subverter, all in one. Hakim was everything and too much. Like a magnet, facing one way I was drawn to him, reversed I was repelled, but there was no other choice, I was in too deeply, my sense of true north lost, the last piece blown away by the flashback. If only I could stay forever in the security of Howie and Eadie's life. No, it was time to go home. I tucked away my fear and faced the inevitable, moving back to our apartment where Hakim had thoughtfully covered the pulsating red walls with a tasteful veneer of off-white.

By the time the police called to let me know Hak was in jail, I knew I had stepped into darkness. While I held the receiver and listened to the officer, I looked at the roll of paper towels hanging neatly above our Formica kitchenette counter. Days earlier, I had watched as Hakim, pleased with his ingenuity, showed me how the cardboard tube inside that same roll was a great hiding place for his stash. He demonstrated with the élan of a salesman, tucking a small bag of heroin into the empty core of our Scott towels, advertised on TV as the solution to all our clean-up problems. Next, grinning mischievously, he added a tiny spoon pilfered from the condiment tray at our favorite Chinese restaurant, "just the right size for snorting," he had assured me, tucking it into his pocket after our meal of steamed dumplings and moo shoo pork. My mind returned to the cop on the other end of the line, alert that this was serious. Had Hak been busted for dope? Was I at risk?

I was pissed. Standing there, listening, I was flooded with images of smoking and using. Marijuana was a way of life for all our friends. I looked over at the paper towels again. Why did Hak always have to take it a step further, and why did I put up with it?

The officer on the phone continued to talk, letting me know I could come down to the station and post bail for Hakim. This did not look like a drug bust. Nothing was amiss. The apartment hadn't been searched. With relief, I assumed the arrest was political, the result of some confrontation in the Hill, fighting to save an evicted family or confronting police brutality. I drove down to the police station and, standing in the reception area, looked up at the officer on duty, ready to do whatever was required. Behind him was an open doorway that led to an unseen corridor extending off to the left. Enraged howls emanated from the end of the hallway. It was Hakim, bellowing, demanding that they un-cage him, powerless except for pride. That was my man. I winced. The cop ignored Hakim's yells, sloughing them off as background Muzak, part of the daily routine at the station. "Are you related to this man?" he asked. "Yes, he's my husband," I lied, fearful they wouldn't release him to me and far too radical to use the word *fiancé*. In the background Hakim continued to rage. He was past words. This injury was too deep for form.

The officer gave me some papers to complete and left the room. Another policeman came through a door at the back herding his drunk, malodorous arrest for the night. I watched as they disappeared down the same hallway that led to Hakim. How did I end up here? In six weeks I would get my master's degree in city planning from Yale. This was not the future I had envisioned on the steps of the Art and Architecture Building.

Drugs continued to infest our life. Hak no longer insisted that I join him but he was clear that he wanted his. Whenever we socialized, Hak was always prepared. Like any thoughtful host or guest, he would pull out his stash with a conspiratorial, welcoming chuckle, generous in his desire to share a good time. Snort a little cocaine, sniff a little heroin, try some psychedelics, it was all good.

Alex, Hak's friend from the Hill, invited us over to dinner. We sat in the living room of his one-bedroom apartment while his wife, Jean, prepared dinner. Alex stretched out his long legs, forming a straight line from his feet through his flowing dashiki to the red, green and yellow crocheted skull cap perched atop his afro. Hakim, short and muscular, tucked stray wisps of hair into his ponytail, grinned and then looked to Alex.

"Hey, man?" he queried, as much with his eyes as with his voice. He reached into his pocket, laughing, took out some powder, and lined it up on the coffee table. "I got a little something. Shall we try it?"

Alex's wife continued to fix dinner. I sat and watched, an afterthought to the ritual. The guys took turns, each snorting a line or two. Heroin is not a social drug. Alex took the first hit. "Good shit," he said. There's nothing like drugs for original dialogue. Hakim snorted his line, leaned back and closed his eyes. "Mmm," he agreed. Another great conversation starter. I crossed my legs and politely waited. Alex got up to vomit first. Hakim followed soon after. That done, they each nodded off, scratching their bellies, privately enjoying their oblivion while I waited for dinner.

Winter settled in along with Adi, the next youngest of Hak's four brothers. Adi was handsome, but I didn't like him. He had the emotional distance of the downer junkie he was. Hakim adored him. Adi's girlfriend was along for the visit. She was petite, Asian, and gorgeous. Not that I saw that much of her. Most of the time, they were both crashed out in our spare bedroom. Up all night, asleep all day, being wasted was all that counted. Like a good hostess, I tried to take it in stride. The times were strange and after all, Adi was Hak's brother. One night, something felt off kilter. I was settled in bed with a good book. Everything was dark except for my small reading lamp. Hakim was hanging out with Adi and his girlfriend in our living room. The whole apartment was still, too still. I put down my book, sat up tall and cocked my ear. Nothing. I took my cup of tea and walked along the unlit hall to our darkened front room. There, in the doorway, I reached for the light switch and gave it a flick. Out of the blackness sprang a freeze frame image. Hak and his brother's girlfriend were going at it on the floor under the tall windows in my living room. They were both naked from the waist down. Her legs were raised. He crouched over her. I smashed down the switch, trying to erase the exposure. Too late! Screaming, I threw my cup of tea across the room and fled out the back door, down the fire escape and over to our neighbors. "Let me in!" I shouted, pounding on their back door. I needed to tell them, to tell anyone what had happened. Crying, jabbering, shorted out, I stood there while they tried to calm me. Hakim jerked open their back door and dashed in. His face was pulled tight. Our neighbors discreetly edged out of the kitchen.

"If you are going to leave, tell me now," he blurted out, looking scared. "What happened was terrible."

Numb, I stood silent, no words in my mouth. Terrible? That's a small word. What I saw was big, too big for such an everyday expression, too big to fit into my brain. Hak looked at me. "I don't want you to go."

I didn't and his brutal, incestuous infidelity was never mentioned again. The light went on, the light went off, and the picture disappeared. Adi moved out. We returned to our daily pace. But something had shifted.

The rest of our life was equally upside-down. I was still a student trying to make sense of school after our aborted coup. Hakim, deep into community organizing, was always on call for the never-ending emergencies that were part of life in the poor black sections of town. He had become Mr. Fixit, constantly trying to put a finger in the dike of chaos caused by poverty and racism. The community was at war with the police and each other. He came in a stranger and with daring and savvy moved right to the center of the action.

Hak had had a long day, most of it fighting to keep a family from being evicted from a public housing project. He arrived home late, fatigued, not sure of the outcome, knowing there was more to do tomorrow and that other emergencies would crop up. I had already eaten but listened solicitously as Hak told me about his day, almost too tired for dinner himself. We went to bed and were awakened at two in the morning by the phone. "It's for you. Someone from the neighborhood," I said and passed him the phone. Hak sat up, listened, and then replied, his voice dispirited, "I'll be right there." Usually a call like this would have him up in a flash, ready to fight the Man, but tonight was different. "I'm tired," Hak sighed. He dressed slowly, moving more with a sense of resignation than the idealistically fueled haste of a few months ago. It's hard to change the world one catastrophe at a time. There had to be a better way. Things were closing in.

I felt the urgency in Hak's voice as he frantically motioned me over to the bedroom window, May Day, 1970. The city was on edge. Activists from across the country were hunkered down in apartments and dormitory rooms ready to demonstrate in defense of Bobby Seale, the leader of the Black Panthers on trial for murder. Jean Genet, Benjamin Spock, Abbie Hoffman, and Jerry Rubin were in town to speak.

"Get a look at this," he said. I could hear rumbling as I approached Hak, the sound unfamiliar but flooding me with dread. Our apartment started to rattle as the noise got closer. I looked out the window and froze. Armored tanks were relentlessly clanking forward. They formed a funereal procession, grinding down the middle of our street, combat ready.

"I was just driving there yesterday," I blurted out.

"Pigs!" Hakim muttered, dropping his side of the curtain and moving away from the window.

I remained, staring out at the overcast morning, all color removed, everything in shades of grey. I had seen this before, but the buildings were always Eastern European and the flags flying were not my own. What was going on? What were we up against? How did the whimsy, optimism and naiveté under which we functioned lead us here? We are more powerful than we think, and we are powerless. The demonstrators in Washington might have put flowers in the sights of the National Guard rifles, but I was going nowhere near these metal monsters. I felt vulnerable and exposed. Yet even then I did not really know how dangerous it could be. Within a few days the knoll at Kent State became our second hillock of shame.

Nixon had just widened the Vietnam War to Cambodia. Students took to the streets, tempers were hot. The governor of Ohio called for the National Guard. By now, some of this was standard procedure, but at Kent State a line was crossed, a covenant broken. Cornered, America turned on its children, its white children. The guard was ordered to fire into the crowd of protesting kids. Four students died and nine were wounded. The myths of safety and a place for us were gone. Where was home?

We talked about leaving New Haven, heading west with friends, building a new world rather than trying to remake the old one. Perhaps the rhetoric of the time was right: change yourself instead of everyone around you.

One thing was clear. This was not how I wanted to live.

# CHAPTER TWO   You've Got a Friend

HAK WAS RAISED IN A LIFE OF WEALTH AND PRIVILEGE. He arrived here when he was ten, his father an appointee to the United Nations. In Jakarta Hak had ridden to school in limousines, a flag flying from the front bumpers. He was a prince, he told me. That sounded good, a bit out of my range but nothing wrong with a little step up. Then the stories got stranger. There was a small alcove in their home in Indonesia that housed a statue. Every night when the family retired the figure faced out. Mysteriously, they awoke each morning to find it turned. "My mother and amah were sure that spirits moved the figurine while we slept," Hakim informed me. I was pretty sure Hak was beyond such primitive thinking, but I did wince when he told me he was circumcised in a traditional ritual when he was twelve. As far as I was concerned this was one step away from scarification and women being banished to menstrual huts to sit on coconuts. All of this was shared as part of our pillow talk. Often, I just listened, impressed and amazed. There were wonderful stories when Hak spoke with pride of his father, a guerilla fighter in the war to liberate Indonesia from the Netherlands. One evening, however, we lay together after making love. Hak started to explain how he was in negotiations involving a ship loaded with cinnamon that was presently anchored off the coast of Singapore. The vessel could not set sail until his terms were met. This was too much for me. I pushed out from under the covers and sat naked on the side of the bed challenging him in disbelief.

"What do you mean you have some ship filled with cinnamon?" I demanded. Who was this man? Was this the stoned delusion of a lunatic or was I just very provincial?

In the states Hak lived in an upscale suburb of New York. As a teen he got a scholarship to a private prep school and then went on to Harvard and Yale. Now, however, he no longer had the protection of a student visa, having risked dropping out of the Asian studies program to work in the Hill. The department of immigration was starting to take note, he told me, tracking dropouts who might be eligible for the draft or political activists who might be out of compliance with their special visas. This was the fulcrum on which my life tipped. There was a chance he could be deported.

Indonesia was dangerous. The summer of Hak's freshman year, he had returned home and done community organizing in a small village. A few years later a purge wracked the country. Over a half-million Communists and left-wing sympathizers were slain in a deranged blood bath, their bodies clogging streams and rivers throughout the country. Right wing gangs impaled the heads of their victims and carried them about on poles. America was where Hakim needed to be and he wanted me with him. Marriage, it seemed, was a necessity if we wanted to be together. There was no doubt I was committed to Hakim. I had made my decision to stay with him and there were no further incidents. We were a couple. Our futures, though vague, held each other. My ambivalence was about the sacrament of marriage itself. "We don't have any choice," he argued. "It's not safe for me in Indonesia. If we don't get married, we may not be able to stay together."

One month after my graduation Hakim and I prepared to exchange our vows in front of a small group of family and friends. He was a handsome Prince Valiant in the blue jacket we worked on together. As a finishing touch I added white gauzy sleeves. When I looked at Hak it all felt right. He was such a part of me. This was a joyous celebration, not a convenience wedding. As I took in everything, what I couldn't see was that too often I chose not to look. I didn't know how.

I learned what it meant to be a woman from my mother, lessons so deep I didn't even know they were there. She idolized my father, hoping for tenderness and affection from a scholar afraid of emotions, a man more at home in the order of abstraction than in the messiness of feelings. I knew her dilemma, even if I couldn't put words to it. In truth, he was right to be cautious. My mother's heart was big, but it could be a yawning cavern, swallowing each of us whole if we didn't watch out. At times, though, my father judged her unfairly. He liked going to the movies, savoring intense foreign films with intellectual themes and great emotional anguish. Often I was his companion. One evening, when I was ten, I proudly headed off to see Charlie Chaplin's angst ridden film *Limelight* with him. I secretly preened that he and I were going, not my mother. As we headed for the door my father made it disdainfully clear that my mother, his wife, was being left behind because she only liked sentimental movies, Walt Disney happy stories, ignoring the fact that the only place he, himself, could tolerate difficult feelings was in books and movies. In real life they broke his heart.

I knew my father loved me deeply, but as a young teen I felt the bite of his derisive, scathing comments every time a love scene intruded on the TV. Sitting cross-legged on the couch in the den, I sucked in the romance on the screen. Leaning forward, my lips open, all my senses alert, not wanting to miss any little detail of love, I confused where the heroine ended and I began. Mmm . . . his tender touch, those caring eyes, such sweet words. Oh yes, this feels good. Me, me, oh please me, I silently wished. "What a load of crap," is what I got. There in the doorway was my dad. I had been caught emotionally masturbating, self satisfying my desire for love. "Yeah, pretty sentimental, should we change the channel?" was all I could muster in reply. Yes, Hakim was the right man for me. He had a high IQ, but not in emotional intelligence. Neither of us did.

Our wedding was a small budget affair. We planned and paid for it ourselves, knowing that immediately after the ceremony we would be heading west in search of a simpler life. Hak and I didn't ask for financial help because we didn't want it. A formal affair with a hall and caterers was never our vision. Luckily so: It would have been difficult to ask our parents to pay after deliberately self destructing our once stellar career prospects by dropping out. No, Hak and I saw our wedding as a great opportunity for simpler, more iconoclastic rituals. Inspired, I contacted a local office supply store and had them make a rubber stamp with the words "Come Celebrate our Conjugal Rites" in a large, no-nonsense font. Next, from the rack of my local Hallmark store, I bought blank cream-colored cards with raised embossed edges, the classiest they had to offer. Now I was ready. Sitting at my kitchen table I hand stamped, front and center, as well as a little askew, fifty invitations and then posted them, smiling all the way to the mail box. With that done, it was time to think about food. As Hak and I were paying, there was no budget or mindset for a sit down meal. I decided on some breads and cheeses. Hak picked out the wine. For a touch of elegance I added melon balls. The night before my wedding, my closest friend Carol and I hand scooped cantaloupes and honeydews, perfecting the trick of flicking our wrists to make perfectly rounded spheres. We filled the tastefully toned, smoky grey plastic lid of the hi-fi set with the melon balls, using it as a serving bowl, and prided ourselves on our ingenuity.

Our justice of the peace, a friend of my parents, was starting to shuffle his papers. In a moment the ceremony would begin. The small gathering of family and friends that convened for our wedding was clustered under a draped parachute hung from the rustic ceiling of a borrowed house. Carol was there along with Clint, her boyfriend. She was tall, about five feet eight, with dark curly red hair, full lips, and a New York accent, somewhat tempered by her drama school education. Outspoken, Jewish, and smart, Carol reveled in the ridiculous, by design and default. She was also disorganized. Chaos followed her. Misplaced items, including her dog, were a way of life. Boredom was anathema. Carol loved to provoke, preferring excitement over tedium. A talented writer, comedienne, and actress, Carol was happiest when performing all her talents simultaneously.

Carol was an unlikely choice for me as a best friend, bold where I was cautious, happy to take dramatic license where I remained wedded to responsible reality. I was incredulous when a few months earlier she confided that she had rewritten her resume awarding herself a fictitious honor from the Yale School of Drama, the Julius Goldberg Award. In reality she had been asked to leave the drama school prior to the end of her final year due to a political run-in with the dean. Carol liked writing her own script and starring in it, even if it did require some significant edits from time to time.

In Carol's life, each and every day presented the chance for a new dramatic persona, no matter where she lived. "Meet me at the Salvation Army," I suggested one afternoon in New Haven. "We're on. See you there," she replied. Not surprisingly, I arrived first. Mounds of used clothes and a slightly stale odor awaited me, each bin a potential fashion gold mine. I lifted a handful of limp sweaters. Where was something to set me off, give me some funk, put some buzz in my step? Glancing up, I saw Carol enter the store, strangely conservative in a brown jersey wrap dress and high-heeled pumps, sporting a shoulder bag. Me, I glimmered in a two-inch choker of emerald sequins, a magenta satin skirt so short it barely covered what it needed to cover, and a yellow stretch-lace, see-through blouse, discovered the week before in this very same store. Carol strode over to me and leaned into my ear. "Today I am Ann Margaret," she whispered conspiratorially. "Well, okay," I thought, dumbfounded, whatever that meant, ignorant of the fact that for an actress every day is a new show, or at least an audition for one.

Just like Jack Sprat and his wife, Carol and I were a study in opposites. Dependable was my middle name. Actually it was my first and last name as well. In seventh grade I was introduced to a brutal rite of adolescence, the slam book, an innocent item transformed into a dangerous weapon that could burn holes in a fragile pre-teen ego. At Durfee Junior High in Detroit our slam book was a green, spiral-bound stenographers' notepad, with flip-over pages. Inscribed on the top of each sheet, in no particular order, was the name of every student in our class, one sheet for each of us. Next came pages dedicated to specific topics such as Most Popular, Best Looking, Smartest, and on down the line. The book was passed around and people, some of them your friends, wrote comments on your sheet— Facebook in the era when camera phones were science fiction. I ended up on the page titled, "Most Likely to Succeed." This was manageable, not too terrible, unless what you really wanted to be was the most beautiful and desired twelve-year-old girl in the whole classroom. On my personal page, "MARGARET GRUNDSTEIN" carefully spelled out in block letters at the top, my best friend wrote, "You can depend on her for an extra pencil whenever you need one . . . and it will always have a good eraser." That, I am sorry to say, just about summed up who I was and who my friends were.

In the summer of 1970 Clint and Carol moved in with us for a month while Carol waited for an acting job in Stockbridge. To help out, Carol frequently washed up after dinner. For Carol, doing the dishes meant a sloppy swipe in lukewarm water followed by a quick rinse. Bits of food and grease were overlooked as she set them to dry in the drainer, busily chatting with me, her attention focused on some foible of Clint's that she gleefully could not wait to recount. Hak liked a drink of water before bed. Passing through the kitchenette he would pick up a tumbler. As he stood there, watching his glass fill, he would let out a deep sigh. His shoulders slumped in frustrated resignation. Dirty again. With bare feet, wearing only loose cotton boxers, he would empty out the drainer and re-wash every glass and dish, a silent judgment leveled against Carol's inherent disarray. Carol never blanched. For her it was a turn at the ridiculous, a humorous face-off that brought spice to life. She was immune to his judgments. If he wanted to rewash everything and make a lot of work for himself, go ahead, was her attitude, embarrassment or an apology nowhere in her lexicon. Hakim was powerful, but Carol didn't care; she would sidestep or even bait him, chuckling all the while. By not taking his pomposity and self-righteousness seriously, she deflated his power, a great defense against a powerful offense, at least until he managed to hit her buttons.

Clint sat next to Carol at the wedding, the two of them a little distance from my parents as everyone waited for the ceremony to begin. I met Clint my first week at Yale. He was six-foot-three with wavy dark hair and a raw country feel that was out of place in the sleek architecture building. This was Clint's first experience in the Northeast. He learned fast. The ill-fitting mustard sport coat he brought with him disappeared after only one wearing and he reverted to his natural attire, Levis. In warm weather you could see the two inch square of mismatched skin on his upper arm, the scar from an old tattoo dedicated to his first wife that was surgically removed before lasers, a time when body art was truly taboo, except of course for sailors.

Clint was from College Station, home of Texas A & M, the middle son of a religious team, his father an Episcopalian minister, his mother the organist, work that as she put it, had "beholden" and "humble" embedded in the job description. All three sons were handsome football heroes, the ultimate currency for young men in the South. After graduating from college in 1959, Clint enlisted for a six-year peacetime tour of duty in the Naval Air Corps, giving him, even in the anti-war climate during which we met, a great deal of unspoken respect. This man, an officer and a pilot, had landed airplanes on heaving flight decks in the middle of turbulent seas, far more than the rest of us had ventured, protected as we were by age, gender, and student deferments. Texan to the core, Clint knew how to be respectful, build anything from scratch, and keep the bad boy out of sight in polite company. Men looked up to him. He was an American cowboy, unflappable and strong, a match for Hakim, whose swagger came from intensity and intellect. During his two years at Yale, Clint roomed with Ken, their houses always a center for radical, uprooted Texas architects as well as unlimited supplies of acid.

Hak and Clint formed an unlikely friendship. In October 1969, our first fall in New Haven, the two of them headed off together for the anti-war moratorium held in New York. Standing together in the doorway of our apartment, anxious to join the fray, Hak was pumped, smiling from ear to ear. Hakim loved politics and confrontation; local, national, international, it didn't matter, he thrived on them all. Hak took a minute to turn and give one more wave good-bye. Next to him, a foot taller and twice the bulk, was Clint, who also stopped and grinned, ready to join but feeling a bit more tentative. This was his first big demonstration. Hak was the leader, the point man in this operation. Clint, for all his heft in size and age, was the acolyte. After six years in the Navy, contradicting the status quo was new to him. Both wore sneakers and jeans, carried light backpacks filled with food and water, and wore red bandanas around their necks in case of tear gas, a regular risk since the 1968 riots at the Chicago Democratic Convention. Carol and I waved and threw kisses. There they were, our guys, outlined by the doorframe, big and small, follower and leader, warriors wearing their colors, united in the thrill of the impending battle. We, their women, stayed home for this one, knowing we would all be going to the big mobilization march on Washington a month later.

Not only were Clint and Carol sharing our apartment, but Clint's youngest brother Stuart was living with us, sleeping on our couch, following his older brother north while adjusting to civilian life after a tour in Vietnam. Stuart was mischievous, an artist in talent and temperament, but down home as well, full of homilies and Southern aphorisms, respectful politeness, and a taste for drink. He followed Clint's lead and joined the service after college, choosing the Air Force instead of the Navy. Unlike Clint, however, Stuart never managed to make pilot, a metaphor for the rest of his life—a flyboy who never got to fly. Women loved him. They found it hard to resist his sweet openness coupled with a sense of humor that could delicately light on an insight and turn it at a rakish angle. Less appealing was his tendency to silently disappear into a brooding darkness as the evening wore on and the quiet sips continued. At the wedding I could see Stuart leaning against the wall behind all the seated guests, nursing a glass of wine. He never liked center stage, preferring the shadows of the wings, especially since his return from Vietnam.

We lived together and helped each other, forming a nucleus, sharing meals and good times and of course a toke here and a snort there for everyone but me. Seeing them as I looked out at the guests, Hakim at my side, knowing Clint and Stuart had hung the parachute that decorated the room, felt good.

There was no walk down the aisle at my wedding. In fact there was no aisle. My mom and dad, along with Hakim's father, were given the respect of occupying front row center. Hak's mother stayed home in Jakarta. I fervently hoped the in-laws would hit it off as I had very little else to offer my father. By choosing not to participate in the medieval ritual where the bride is given away, I relegated him to the role of just another guest. My parents did their best to be upbeat and hide the horrified feelings that threatened to overwhelm them, while my beloved Aunt Nelma secretly wished that I was marrying that soft-spoken, sweet, southern Stuart instead. During the ceremony it poured rain. Instead of a honeymoon we went home and packed for a different trip to nirvana, our drive west. Clint, Carol, Stuart, and a few other friends were to meet up with us in Eugene, Oregon.

Within a week we headed out, our old life behind us. Hak had traded in the BMW for a white van. He stripped it down, making room for our bed, a plywood platform. Underneath we stashed boxes filled with everything we owned. We were ready to make the leap into trust like all the dreamers before us, Hak leading, me following. Oregon was our goal. Simply arriving there was in and of itself the plan, at least as far as I knew. Money? Jobs? We would deal with that later. Escape was as far as our vision took us, and that felt good enough to me. I needed to leave.

# PART II

## Greenleaf

# CHAPTER 3    People Get Ready

LEV, AN OLD CHILDHOOD FRIEND OF HAK'S, accompanied us. In truth, it might be more accurate to say that I accompanied them, as it often felt like they were the couple and I was the extra. Lev didn't like me. Then again, Lev didn't like most people. He was taciturn, with dark eyes that glowered out at the world from behind his black beard. I gave him wide berth, which was not difficult as he rarely spoke to me.

On our way west, we stopped in Cleveland for a visit with my parents, my first time home as a married woman. I could feel that things had changed. Hak was now the man in my life. Nine years ago I had seen it happen at my sister's wedding. My father walked her down the aisle, handed her off to Bruce, her new protector, and then headed for the sidelines, the natural course of things, even in a feminist world. My problem was that I had been passed on to my husband, but Hak seemed to have dropped the baton. He was nowhere in sight. Hak and Lev were holed up in our van at the end of my parent's driveway, their ad hoc headquarters. Under the guise of making small repairs, they huddled inside, smoked dope, and avoided my family. As politicos, they were committed to a new and better future and would not compromise by hanging out with the enemy. Or perhaps they were just rude. The difference was no longer clear.

Inside the house I ran interference, trying to placate both my parents and my husband. It came to a head at dinner the second night we were there. My mother made an elaborate family meal of brisket, roasted potatoes, herbed green beans, and fresh strawberry pie. She sat poised at her end of the table near the swinging kitchen door. My father claimed his spot at the other end, the head of the table. They each had matching polished captain's chairs anchoring the magnetic poles of our dining room. I sat in between them in one of the lesser chairs. Hak was opposite me with Lev at his side. During the meal, Lev managed to enthusiastically devour his share while simultaneously exuding contempt for the people who graciously fed him. Sated, he stepped outside to smoke a cigar, leaving without a thank you or any offer to help clear up the remains. That left Hak behind enemy lines without any back-up.

I loved eating together. It was a strong part of our family tradition. My mother dominated the first part of the meal with her cooking. As dinner and our maturity progressed, my father took center stage, adored by my mother as well as the rest of us. Smart, charming, scholarly, funny, whimsical, and warm when he wasn't defended and distant, he was the pinnacle of our family, my mother the roots. Grundy would lean back in his chair, stretch his legs and then, ever the professor, toss out a provocative idea to get things going, especially if we had guests. This evening Hak sat like a respectable son-in-law, not quite gracious, but lacking overt hostility. I let my guard down and relaxed into the discussion phase of the meal. The conversation turned to Vietnam. My father, taking his usual role, threw out a salvo.

"What is it you want with all your marches and rallies?" he asked, sitting back expectantly. From old habit I went on alert, feeling the assault, my father's familiar use of the accusatory and dismissive pronoun "you." With that it became personal, not a discussion but an attack, my father against the other side, the provocative professor safe at the head of his seminar, everyone else, rightly or wrongly, tossed by him into a position of disdain. Only as an adult did I began to understand why I got so riled up in discussions with him.

Tonight, however, was different. My father didn't know he had miscalculated. Hak was not one of his polite students.

"Nixon needs to end the war." Hak countered, still civil. "The domino theory is an excuse. Vietnam is a civil war, more about colonialism and self rule, than a threat to the free world."

"You people are naïve," my father parried.

Hak seemed less bothered by the debate than the hot topic grenade revealed underneath. His back straightened and he jerked forward, ready to lob it back.

"You mean you support Nixon?"

My head turned from Hak at one end of the table to my father at the other. This discussion had gone from civil to incendiary before a dessert dish had even been cleared.

"He's the right man for the job. The United States must remain strong."

Even I was surprised. My father had voted for Tricky Dick? I had been raised in a liberal household. My mother was active in Democratic politics. She went as an alternate delegate to the convention in Chicago where Kennedy was nominated. What happened?

"Nixon," Hakim snorted derisively.

"Peace and love are not going to stop the Communists," was my father's arch reply.

Hak glared, stood up, and slammed his open hand on the bare wood of the table. "Fascist!" he spat out in disgust, then turned and strode through the swinging door into the kitchen and out to the van. My parents and I were shocked into silence, too embarrassed to look at each other. I had ducked during the sniping, but now I needed to act. What did my father think of me, of our plans to throw aside everything I had achieved under his tutelage? He was always thrilled when I took risks, but it also scared him. Temperamentally we were very much alike. No, I didn't need to know. I had married my husband. Without looking at my parents I rose, pushed back my chair, and left the table. The time had come to move on.

We camped our way across country, three of us in our converted van. Within a few nights we found ourselves in the vast empty spaces of northern New Mexico. As dusk approached, we pulled off the road into a campground that consisted of one lone picnic table and two trees. Flat ranch land extended past the horizon in all directions with no animals or humans in sight. I stood for a moment, taking in the scale of the landscape, before turning my attention to dinner. Hak and Lev unloaded our food and set up the Coleman stove. While I cooked, they made a campfire. After dinner, Hak and Lev warmed themselves by the fire and shared a joint. I lingered by the table, lost in my own thoughts, wiping out the camping pots and packing up our food.

"Do you think you'd ever move back to Jakarta?" Lev asked.

"Maybe" Hak replied, taking a toke and making a thumbs-up sign. He passed the joint to Lev, coughing. "But right now I like it here."

"Yup," Lev agreed, sucking in the smoke.

"Actually," Hak laughed, "that's why I went to graduate school. I was afraid of being deported. But once the law on asylum passed, my studies were over."

Lev was confused. "What did that have to do with you?"

"Man, I was in danger. I had done some organizing in a rural village."

"I still don't get it."

"Whack," Hak exclaimed, abruptly slicing the air with his hand. "There are a lot of dead lefties in Indonesia."

I couldn't hear everything, only bits and pieces. Hak went on about some United Nations protocol that protected refugees from persecution in their home countries, explaining that the United States had ratified the treaty our first fall in New Haven. Then it hit me. That was when Hak dropped out of graduate school, when he became involved in community organizing.

I stood there, camping pot in one hand, paper towel in the other, slowing absorbing the impact of this information. Hak knew. He knew all along there was no risk of deportation. When he pressured me to marry him, arguing that he would be kicked out of the country if we didn't, it was a lie. The asylum law protected him. Cold comfort that Hak had lied to persuade me and not to protect himself. Or perhaps marriage was just an extra-added precaution. I had no idea. All I knew was that Hak had manipulated me. I hadn't felt compelled to marry. He did. Why? I had no idea. Once again, whatever Hakim wanted, Hakim got. I stood there in the vast scrub of New Mexico, stunned. What did this mean about our marriage? Maybe nothing, I reasoned. Ours was not a green card union. I never believed it was. We both wanted to be together and I needed him, especially after my acid flashback. We were married. We loved each other. That was enough. I chose to ignore the chasm that had just cracked open beneath me. The light went on. The light went off. This time I didn't even scream.

Once we hit Eugene, Hak and I, along with Lev, rented an apartment that became the forward base for all our friends. Clint stayed with us as he jumped between coasts, hoping to persuade Carol, who was still wedded to her acting career, to commit to a new future. Don, an undergraduate friend of Clint's, followed. He was a native of Eugene and had talked us all into the glories of the Pacific Northwest. His parents, a generous couple, opened their home to us when we first arrived. Don was a lot like his parents, warm and solid, but he had an extra dollop of something, a strong sense of adventure, that took him places his father's work as a high school principal never could. Mary Ellen, Don's girlfriend, was also a local. They had been together since high school and were a study in contrasts. Don was a work in browns, grounded like the earth, with thick auburn hair, dark eyes, and a dense beard. Mary Ellen was his opposite, blond and blue eyed with a childlike quality that seemed to miss a beat. You could feel it in the singsong cadence of her speech and in her penchant for walking on her toes. She was devoted to Don.

Don's presence was also a draw for Roggie, another undergraduate from Yale. Roggie was precise, brilliant, and disciplined, a dedicated altar boy until he went to college. Physically he had the whippet-thin body of a gymnast. Temperamentally he had the need to wander, unattached to anything but an idea. Unlike the rest of us, Roggie came from more working class roots. His father was a Dallas policeman and his mother, a seamstress, helped out the family financially, wearing out several sewing machines making all the clothing for his four sisters. There were six children all living together in a three-bedroom, GI Bill tract home. After being the first in his family to go to college, Roggie threw it all away, dropping out of Yale to travel. The student strikes and occupation of the campus by the National Guard helped jump-start his natural proclivities. All course work had unraveled and by default, finals were cancelled for many spring 1970 classes. When Roggie looked at the young Guardsman protecting his campus, he saw more similarities than differences in their backgrounds. If not for his brilliance and a lot of luck, he could have been wearing the military uniform that held the line, rather than the scruffy clothes of a student protestor. Roggie left school and headed west, never abandoning the scholar within him, just moving to less formal educational pastures.

Clint's friend Guy, another architect from Texas, moved in with us for part of the winter. He was tall and lanky and had a "Howdee" greeting that opened many doors. The real kicker, though, was his mischievous grin. He had spirit. You could feel it in his customized VW bug. Guy had stripped it down, tearing out the back seat to make room for his tools and a very small sleeping platform. The outside gleamed in shiny, metal flake blue. Guy had cut through the roof and added an orange Plexiglas dome that protruded in the shape of a five-pointed star, the distinctive insignia of his home state. Add one Texas decal, and Guy, as the Lone Rainbow, was ready to take on America. His base was the couch in our living room in Eugene. We received him with enthusiasm, his parents in Austin with more trepidation. They made it clear that with his long hair and beard he was not welcome, which was later amended to the understanding that if he was going to visit, it needed to be under the cover of night.

We converged in Oregon but lacked a strategy. My solution was to cook. The Giant Zucchini, a tiny vegetarian restaurant tucked in the Y, needed a pastry chef. Twice a week I bicycled to their kitchen and baked. The arrangement was a trade. They provided clientele and ingredients. I volunteered skill and inspiration. This was my first time cooking commercially and I saw it as an opportunity to experiment. Hippie food didn't have to be heavy. Why not natural and gourmet? Galvanized, I used the richest, darkest molasses I could buy for my ginger cookies, each bite filled with chopped pieces of candied ginger that went off like sparklers on your tongue. Flaky whole-wheat pastry dough was a challenge. I met it head-on, making lime curd tarts that balanced the nuttiness of whole grain against the sweet tang of the filling. This was fun. Hak and Lev, however, were still at loose ends, politicos without a constituency. Unbeknownst to me, they cooked up their own scheme.

We had been in Eugene a month when Hak informed me that he and Lev were going out. They made it clear that I wasn't invited. I consoled myself with the thought that tomorrow was a baking day at the Giant Zucchini and I needed to get to bed early. When I awoke the next morning, Hak was asleep next to me. Lev had crashed in his room next door. Knowing they were tired, I tiptoed around the apartment, taking my long skirt, hiking boots, and sweater into the living room so I could dress without waking them. Outside, I grabbed my bike and rode to the Y. When I returned home, I found Hak and Lev sitting around, smoking a joint.

"What did you guys do last night?" I asked, wanting to catch up on the news from my husband.

"We were out," Hak said, shrugging his shoulders. Lev glanced over at him.

"Hey guys, I know you were out. Did you go drinking or run into someone we know?"

"We were looking around."

"Looking around? What do you mean? For what?"

"Margaret, we were out. Leave it at that."

"No, Hak. I don't want to leave it at that. You and Lev are thick as thieves, and here I am outside it all. I don't like it. What's going on?"

Hakim stood his ground, silent. Lev matched him. I could feel they were united in a way that excluded me and exuded danger. Lev, cool and impenetrable, pulled out a cigar and slowly rolled it between his thumb and fingers. He glanced over at Hak, made eye contact, and then looking directly at me, announced in a flat voice that carried a challenge: "We liberated some explosive devices. They're temporarily being stored here."

They weren't asking, they were confronting, the privilege to decide exclusively theirs.

"No, you don't," I countered. "I live here too." I turned to Hak, knowing there was nothing I could say that would penetrate Lev's disdain for me. "Who do you think we are? The Weathermen?" Instantly, extreme radical politics, which before had seemed slightly romantic, became anathema, the risk and brutality beyond my ken, especially in what I knew was my pretty wonderful life. I looked around, searching for something that might look like a detonator. Inside Lev's bedroom I could see a metal box on the floor.

"Get that thing out of here," I demanded, pointing into Lev's room. Neither of them moved. Lev watched, still holding his cigar, his eyes catching Hak's from time to time. Everyone knew about the Weathermen, well-educated middle class kids like us, except a few had blown themselves up while making pipe bombs in a New York City townhouse. Those that survived the blast were now fugitives. I was not in this for violence. Peace and love? Sure. Living in harmony with the earth? Great. I could sign on for those. They were part of my nature. Explosives were different. A line had been crossed.

Lev turned and went into his room, leaving the clear impression of his distaste. Hak was left with me.

"Hak, get that shit out of here," I demanded. I had hit my limit.

The problem was it made no difference. Hakim got his jacket and left the apartment, returning later that night. Nothing more was said until a few days later. Lev was out visiting his girlfriend, Brandi. Hak and I sat on the well-worn couch that came with our furnished rental. He was watching the news on television. I half listened, most of my attention on the beret I was crocheting for Hak out of second hand yarn from Goodwill.

"Hak," I said. "I don't like having that detonator and whatever else you liberated in the house."

He remained focused on Walter Cronkite, who was narrating clips of napalm bombs falling on Vietnam, but turned to me briefly to reiterate his stand.

"Lev and I have it under control. This isn't anything that involves you."

My hands stopped mid-stitch. "Of course this involves me. I could be arrested."

I got up and paced around the room. Hak, done with the conversation, turned his attention back to the explosions on TV.

That was it. I snapped inside. What did he mean, this doesn't involve me? Don't you dare not talk to me. Where do you get off, motherfucker? Where is some empathy? What about a little planning together? How come it's always you and not me? I lunged at him and grabbed his shirt.

"Listen to me, just listen to me!" I screamed.

Shocked, he pulled back. Buttons flew off his chest. I had torn his shirt open. Scared, I let go. Hak moved toward the door, ready to leave, not saying a word.

My mind raced. How do I get through to this man? Where is the partnership in this marriage? Can't he at least discuss the issue with me, yes me, not Lev? Don't write me off as the anxious little woman. This isn't about fear, it's about morals. I know the difference. Who are we? How could he even think about crossing the line into violence?

I grabbed the heavy glass ashtray on the coffee table and heaved it as hard as I could, aiming to make some sort of impact. Hak was agile. He had been a wrestler. Deftly, he stepped aside. The ashtray hit the wall, bounced off and thudded onto the matted carpet. Hakim turned and walked out the door.

How did we get here? I had just hurled a chunk of glass at my husband, wanting to hurt him as much as he was hurting me. How was I supposed to penetrate his self- assured armor? Hak was always the leader, always right, never in need of outside counsel. Great for war, but this was a marriage.

Hak came back later that night and we made up in bed. The next evening, at dinner, he told me they had disposed of the detonator. There was no explanation offered, just the fact that it was gone. I didn't push. How or where they got rid of their lethal bonanza didn't matter. We were back on track. I didn't really believe he had changed his mind because of my anger, but I was grateful and relieved nonetheless. Hak had gotten lost in the confusing maze of political resistance. Violence was not his way. Clearly we needed some direction.

# CHAPTER 4  Our House

"WHAT FARM? WHERE?" I SPUTTERED, FEELING anxiety rise like a heat-seeking missile. "Time to make a move," Hakim delightedly informed me. "We found the perfect place. There's room for all of us."

All of us? As newlyweds, I still held onto the hope that all of us were two of us. My dream was to dump Lev. The other rotating guests were fine as long as they remained guests and rotating, separate but not equal in my relationship with Hak. He, it seems, had different plans. Hak, Don, and Roggie saw a rental ad for a farm located an hour outside Eugene. They checked it out and decided the property was just what we needed, a concept that was not quite clear, but the idea of moving in together seemed right to everyone, or at least everyone but me.

"Why can't we stay here?" I argued. "I like having my own apartment. How will we have our own home if we share with everyone?" Putting aside my dreams about marriage and my hopes for sweet intimacy was hard. Like every girl, I grew up with romantic fantasies. Where was the honeymoon in our relationship? Why couldn't Hakim plan with me, instead of for me? Was he was afraid I would hobble him? Probably. Yes, I needed a push, some pressure to help me cross the threshold of my apprehension. Hak moved at a more radical pace, bold in the service of his own needs, unfettered by anything else. Sometimes it was great, forcing me to loosen up. Other times it wasn't. Hak's push could often feel like a shove. This time he was right. We were on the cusp of a great adventure. Without him I would not have made the leap.

"The lease is for a year," he said. "We'll have our own room where we can be together." My response softened. I certainly was not staying behind, and it was pretty clear everyone else was moving ahead. Actually I started to perk up at the thought of a garden, forested hills, and rolling pastures. I knew Hak always landed on his feet. The farm might be fun.

Goodbye Armageddon, hello Paradise. Greenleaf, Oregon, became my new communal home. With the move we stepped onto the stage of our new life. All "can'ts" and "don'ts" were left behind. The dark urban America of the last few years was long gone. We were ready for adventure. When else if not now, when we were beautiful just by being young and anything still seemed possible.

"Well, look at this," I said as we approached the farm in Greenleaf. We bumped across a rickety wooden bridge that had no railings, only a pile of boards loosely laid out, side by side, arching over the fast moving creek below. A winding dirt road led away from the water, bordered on both sides by ten-foot-tall, wild blackberry vines. Beyond these tangled hedgerows were mowed pastures and then our new home, a ranch house set in the middle of ten acres.

We were in a protected little valley holding three distinct homesteads with ours nestled in the center. Green was everywhere—towering, mounded, stacked, and spread; grasses, trees, needles, and leaves; dark, light, dappled, and dense. We had entered the technicolor of our own secret garden. Our fortune, however, was built on someone else's loss. We rented from a family that could no longer afford to farm. The dad had taken a job in town to support his family of four. Roggie told me later it was clear their decision was neither an easy nor a happy one. He explained that after signing the rental agreement, he, Don, and Hak stood around on one side of the living room while the owners and their children clustered together near the opposite wall, subdued, small talk over. Everyone was uncomfortable. The young son, about ten, stood next to his dad. Echoing his father's stance, the boy had his hand in his pocket, elbow out, his body sad and slouched. Together they formed a repeated refrain. For our guys it was a difficult moment, forcing into relief some unwanted truths. We "poor hippies" were richer than a working farmer.

Having taken possession, the next step was to settle in. Hakim and I took one of the upstairs rooms. Don and Mary Ellen claimed the bedroom next door. Clint, always the elder statesman of the group, staked out the separate, small structure to the side of the house in the hope that its privacy might placate Carol and seduce her into returning from New York and staying past the easy days of spring and summer. She had come west with all of us, but after a month returned to her subsidized artist's loft in the Village, intent on establishing herself as an actress. Clint, however, was ready to make the move. Country was his place of comfort. He worked with his hands. Tools were his natural medium. Together they had talked of buying land in Oregon, but Carol envisioned it as a haven to visit, a counterpoint to New York. Clint saw it as home and wanted her along. He made several visits back to Manhattan, trying to persuade Carol to join him. When she resisted, he loaded his battered Ford Falcon and headed to Greenleaf without her. Now Carol faced a real dilemma, a choice between her man and her career. Clint knew what he was doing. Carol had trouble making decisions, jumping sides until circumstances forced her to choose. Even then, as those around her sighed with relief, she proposed plans for reversing course. In the end, Clint acted, Carol followed, subletting her Westbeth subsidized artist loft, just in case.

Most of the men in our group, being architects, regarded every physical environment as a work in progress. The ranch house lost its suburban feel as each man scavenged and sawed, their hammers bringing our vision into focus. Money was tight. We didn't buy beds, we built them; boxy platforms quickly put together from rough pieces of wood. Any living room furniture we had reflected the same aesthetic. Draped parachutes softened our bedrooms. Doors disappeared from their frames. We celebrated the open and shared quality of our new living situation. Imaginations ran loose, but reality impinged with the knowledge that as renters, and responsible ones at that, we were living in someone else's house. Our creative energy needed additional sites and canvases.

"Hey come take a look at this," Don called out. Hak and I left our room and gathered in the upstairs hallway along with Guy and his girlfriend Janet. Don, barefoot and bare-chested, was holding a colored marker, his expression low-key behind his beard. Mary Ellen, in contrast, was naked, balanced on her tiptoes, grinning with pride. She was on display, covered from neck to knee in drawings. Looking closer, and aided by an annotated dialogue from Don, I saw that Mary Ellen sported a complete comic strip on her body. There it was, frame by frame, undulating over the curves of her breasts and belly, in full color, text included, a living underground comic. She giggled while Don walked us through his creation. Mary Ellen had become Don's muse and medium all in one.

Warmer weather opened up possibilities, especially as room in the house was limited. Lee, another architect from Houston, arrived in late spring. He was the first to claim an outside space, building a sleeping platform just a few feet above the forest floor. I walked to the woods at the back of the property and found him stretched out and stoned in his open-air crèche. Lee had nailed old boards onto the decaying remains of a massive fir, making a raised pallet that formed the centerpiece of his new home. Young seedling trees were the walls, their branches an arched ceiling, while underfoot leaves and fir needles served as entryway carpeting. Five-foot-high ferns added texture and fill, providing intimacy as well as a foil for discretely hidden piles of clothing and supplies. Plastic sheeting draped overhead like the gauzy scarves of faeries, offering protection from the dew that settled at night. It was an illustration straight out of a children's book where precious little critters lived under the spread of mushroom caps, everything cobbled together with ingenuity and charm, just bigger. In the center of all this, reclining against a bolster of blankets and pillows like a pasha of the pines, was Lee, his languid form one with all around him. He greeted me from his prone position and, like any proud homeowner, extolled the virtues of his dwelling, pointing out design nuances that evoked little cries of delight from me. I stretched out on the other end of the platform and politely refused a toke while Lee inhaled deeply. We chatted while I relaxed, completely captivated. It was an art exhibit, but one lacking in self-conscious artifice. Eat your heart out, galleries. Forget hoping to transcend reality through works on the wall. We were artists, living in our installations, set in the garden of God's creation. I took it all in, clucking and complimenting Lee on each whimsical detail, basking in the reflected glory of his work.

Aren't we great, I thought as I walked back across our pasture, feeling buoyed and blessed, confusing myself, the patron, with the artist and his creativity. In actuality, my home was our snug room in the ranch house, my doubt about communal living having vanished with the move. Everything was once again in place. What I didn't realize was that I was one beat behind. Arboreal living was the next frontier.

Hakim was not an architect, but he knew a good thing when he saw it. He decided we needed a tree house. Once again he brought me up short. Who does he think I am? I am not going to live my life in some branches. What about my things? Let Lee live outside if he wants to. What will I do if I have to pee at night? While I thrashed around Hakim acted, wisely letting me tire myself out. He built a sleeping platform fifteen feet high in the branches of an alder and we moved out of the house and into the woods, finally a place of our own, perfect, although a little damp at night.

Happily settled in our new love nest, Hak and I lay back, nestled together, suspended in leaves and sunlight, floating in time and space, a quiet afternoon at home.

"Howdee," came Guy's signature greeting.

I looked over the edge of our platform and saw Guy and his girlfriend Janet. She was an old friend he invited to visit, and now they were a couple, a somewhat loose concept in Guy's mind. Janet was a long, tall Texan, blond and blue-eyed, with a natural intelligence and reserve that generated respect. She was quiet and careful in her speech, rarely thrown off her center, and up for more than one might have thought.

They were a-calling, out on a leisurely stroll, stopping by to visit. What a nice neighborly feel. Only, look at that, they were both stark naked! Who went visiting neighbors without any clothes on? How could you just walk around like you did in normal life, in front of other people and each other, on an afternoon constitutional, but without a stitch of clothing? Swimming together naked, that was different. But this was nudist-colony naked, doing everyday things in the all together. In retrospect it was more like the Garden of Eden naked, but I didn't know that until later.

I did know that I shouldn't show any shock or surprise. Hakim, of course, was way too cool to do double takes.

"Come on up," he called out. "We're just hanging out." Guy and Janet obliged. They climbed our ladder; straight up the slats nailed into the side of our tree, with Guy's bare booty in Janet's upturned face. They seemed okay with it. Matter of fact, everyone but me seemed unfazed. I decided to go along. And I did. We had a very suburban visit, our guests balanced in the boughs of our tree, us dressed, them not, with no one saying a thing about it.

# CHAPTER 5 Let's Get Together

SUMMER, ENDLESS SUMMER, HAD ARRIVED and our generation was on the road looking for something better. Morning Star, New Buffalo, The Farm—these were some of the names that beckoned, communes that seemed to promise the dawning of that ephemeral concept, the Age of Aquarius, heralded in the musical *Hair*, where the rapture of peace and love will prevail in the universe. We were children of the times and the grandchildren of past utopians. Greenleaf became a stop on the underground map that marked these longings; tribal tales passed through word of mouth.

Lenny, one of many visitors, appeared unexpectedly, part of a random group of seekers traveling west in an old school bus. He was seventeen, on his own and fleeing suicide, the bus his way out. His mother had died three years before and nothing had gone well since. Lenny rechristened himself Rocky, a name full of fight, and started what he hoped would be a new life. There were six people on the bus including a past liaison of Clint's, hot on his scent, and an ex-computer geek who unfurled spools of liberated magnetic tape from the windows, casting out technology in his wake. Rocky noted that it was a grand symbolic gesture, but ultimately did little but add to the roadside litter. Money was a problem, especially when halfway across the country Rocky ran out of funds and became dependent on the group. His bus mates, torn between the hippie ethic of sharing and the reality of financial pressures, said nothing but silently counted every bite of food he ate.

Rocky's only hope, which got more fragile with every mile, was to make it to San Francisco. Life was closing in again. Then came the day he stood at the foot of the Continental Divide, their massive peaks rising out of the plains, stacked against the clear blue sky, marking the line between him and the West ahead of him. Rocky, overcome, sat down in the scrubby roadside grass, put his head on his knees, and cried. He had never seen mountains before. For him, the sun had risen and set in the urban canyons of New York City. Now here were the Rockies: majestic, grand, eternal. Three days later, transformed, he crossed our bridge.

All our big decisions were made at the dining-room table and this one was no different. "Hey guys," Hakim repeated several times, standing up, trying to get everyone's attention. We were done eating and slowly quieted, wanting to hear what Hak had to say.

"You all know Rocky," he said. We nodded while he paused to claim the moment. "His friends on the bus are ready to head on down to San Francisco." Alert, we waited for the point. "I have been hanging out with Rocky the past few days, smoking, talking, just enjoying things. He's gotten to like it here, and I think it would be great if he stayed with us instead of moving on." There it was, on the table. Coming from Hak, this was less a request than an edict waiting to be ratified. Rocky sat to Hak's left, his age obscured by his full dark beard and his billowing mass of curly hair tied back into a loose pony tail. There was, however, no mistaking his need, as his bright eager puppy eyes scanned the table.

"I'll understand if you don't want me." He smiled, apologetic and nervous. "I'd like to stay and help out and live here. I know you can't just let anyone in and I'll figure something out if you say no, but the bus isn't working for me, and this place feels really good."

Clint responded first, always low-key, never quite front on. "Things are getting full. When summer ends, space is going to get kind of tight."

Hakim parried, taking the high road, "We have tons of room. If we trust, things always work out." he argued. "Rocky needs a place to stay and he already fits in." His points were pretty basic. Hak's genius was in the presentation. This was not done behind closed doors or in the privacy of small group discussions. No, it was done with Rocky at the table, seated beside his mentor, anxiously awaiting fate's call, tensed to absorb one more punch, but hoping for a reprieve if not salvation. You could feel Rocky's hunger and his hurt.

There was no vote, no decisive minute, just a bit of back and forth with Hak at the helm. We moved on to dessert. Thumbs up thumbs down, black ball, white ball, open border or closed immigration, we faced the same problem just different rules. Rocky was now one of us.

The next day Hakim picked up the keys to Guy's Volkswagen and rounded up Rocky. "Come on," he gestured, grinning broadly. "Let's go spend some money." They went into town where Hakim treated Rocky to a raincoat and a few other items. This was how we lived, equal and accepted, in theory at least. Rocky knew otherwise. He was young, uneducated, and broke. What could he offer? Where did he fit in? Rocky was dependent on the mantle of protection provided by Hak, making him one of us, but not quite, a little like Mary Ellen. This was the unspoken conflict at the core of Rocky's stay; should he believe the rhetoric or the small daily slights. Were we the bus, just somewhat nicer?

When Rocky arrived, Hak and I were living in our tree house. That left a room, our room, in the main building vacant except for a few cardboard boxes holding our downsized possessions, a logical spot for Rocky to settle. A few days after the bus left, I went upstairs to dig out an extra pair of jeans. When I opened the door I saw my cartons neatly stacked in the corner. On the floor at the side of the bed were two scuffed work boots leaning against each other. An open sleeping bag covered our plywood bed. Rocky relaxed on top of it, his legs crossed at the ankles, arms folded behind his head. "What's he doing here?" I thought, annoyed that he looked so at home.

"Why is all your stuff in my room?" I challenged. "Hak and I live here. See those boxes. They're ours." Rocky knew he was on tentative ground. He nervously jumped off the bed and faced me, his eyes vulnerable with fear. "I'm sorry. I didn't know. I'll find someplace else, but everything is taken," he said, trying to appease me and explain his dilemma at the same time.

He was right. The space did look empty. Hak and I had moved most of our belongings to our pied-à-terre in the boughs of a sixty-foot alder. I had envisioned returning when the leaves and Visqueen became inadequate as shelter. But I knew I couldn't hold the bedroom vacant as insurance for the fall. No one would have supported me, least of all my husband. The pragmatics of the situation became clear. I needed to yield. "You could have asked," I chided, capitulating to the social realities. Months later Rocky told me that he had been thinking, "Shit. I didn't even know you lived in this room. One thing about this place, for a commune it is not very communal." Rocky's survival instincts tempered his response. They served him well.

Rocky settled in as well as Lev's girlfriend, Brandi, whom he met in Eugene. She was a woman waiting for a man, hoping for a baby and looking for an easy ride in the seemingly forgiving world where peace, love, and welfare intersected, and no one cared that your education ended at high school. The story was an old one, the context contemporary. Brandi brought her friend Fairchild with her, a quiet, gentle woman, who, like her long skirts and full breasts, flowed with whatever was happening, and for a while that was Guy. Fairchild was open to sex in what appeared to be the hippie ideal: unattached, no expectations, a natural process. She drifted. Coupling was part of the current. It was a powerful draw for Guy. Janet, Guy's real girlfriend, stayed in the background, but not out of the picture.

Who was with who became even more complicated with our next additions. Guy brought Gerald, a conscientious objector, along with his girlfriend, Lisa, into our circle. He met them camping before we moved to the farm. Lisa's gentle face was beatific, moon-shaped with round eyes. She wore her blond hair in heavy braids that sweetly crowned her head like a pure Norwegian princess. Years before the concept of spirituality became fashionable, Lisa carried its essence within her and it was unmistakable. She radiated kindness and light and softness. Gerald carried the same essence as Lisa but in the masculine, with a slightly more ascetic feel. He had a slender build, a long brown beard and hair to match. Both were followers of Yogi Bajan, not quite Sikhs but most often clothed in white. Together they exuded a vital force connected to universal goodness. Being with them was always comforting.

Carol had returned for the summer, torn between Clint and career, not an easy decision to make. Should she be an actress or a writer? Los Angeles or New York? Liberal or radical? Certainly these were life-changing choices, but Carol's inability to be decisive complicated the process. One thing on which Carol was clear was that she and Clint wanted to purchase land. None of us were concerned. Property sounded like a good idea. Where it would lead was unclear but "go with the flow," and "it will all work out" were our functional mantras.

Carol arrived at Greenleaf to find old friends, new faces, and big changes. No longer were we a loose collection of well-educated strivers, certified for success. We had morphed into a commune, our members crossing every socio-economic boundary, arriving through word of mouth, as well as invitation.

Skeptical of living with drop-outs and strangers, Carol kept her emotional distance. Drama, however, seduced her. Every day at Greenleaf was a happening; steam baths, communal dinners, animal slaughters, and the celebration of celestial events. Carol thrived on breaking boundaries, thrilled when life overflowed the straight and narrow. We could meet her there. In June, five months after our arrival at Greenleaf, we decided that the upcoming solstice was a great opportunity to host a celebration and further expand our network. Carol and Clint had discovered two sister communes, Footbridge and Three Rivers, while exploring on Clint's motorcycle. We invited them to our party. Three Rivers was the most rustic, not due to any philosophic stance, but the result of poor construction skills and bad judgment. One of their members had left a candle unattended and it burned down their rented cabin. Now they lived in three tents and the two small huts they had managed to cobble together on the same land, after persuading their landlord to let them stay. Like us, they had a very loose social structure with no dominant philosophy or leader. Footbridge, in contrast, had several rough-hewn buildings scattered over their forested acreage and strong leadership in the form of Johnny and his woman, Tchanan, known in her former life as Karen. Johnny was lithe, lean, and dark, a Jew who merged Semitic with Sioux and integrated kosher slaughter of their livestock with Native American blessings before dinner. Footbridge came the closest to being self-sufficient. They raised their own meat, made their own cheese, had the best garden, and canned to tide them over. All this was done with drama, ritual, and off the grid. They were living theatre. Carol loved them.

We at Greenleaf, with our ranch house, pastoral land, and comfortable utilities, were a little soft. Maybe we didn't use our dishwasher out of respect for a philosophic stance, but we had one. We also had hot and cold running water, one flush toilet, a shower/bath, and electricity. For all of us the common dream was a hybrid of Native American hunter-gatherers crossed with pioneer homesteaders, ignoring the irony that was inherent in the combination. Who was the purest of them all in the quest to step lightly on this earth? Footbridge came closest. We brought up the rear. At Greenleaf, however, in spite of our amenities, we did hold one strong trump card. Our men were architects. They knew how to build. That brought us a great deal of respect.

The day of our solstice celebration was sunny and warm and I was excited about meeting new friends. Like any good hostess I prepared for our guests by cooking. Footbridge arrived first. I heard greetings and left the kitchen to meet them, wiping my hands on my makeshift apron, a torn tee shirt tucked into the waistband of my jeans. One look outside and I abruptly pulled it off, discarding anything that might make me look like a housewife, even a funky one. Across my line of vision paraded Amazons, tall and confident, boldly striding through the stubble of our backyard.

The Footbridge women had arrived. They were dark in mien, dusky in color, and perfumed by a touch of wood smoke.

I'm in trouble, was my thought. These women have knives. Not jaunty Swiss Army ones with miniature scissors and a can opener, but serious weapons with wooden hafts and six-inch blades set in leather sheaths tied to their thighs. What *were* these warriors of the woods doing with knives and how come I didn't have one? Never have I felt more poorly accessorized in my life. They oozed bravado. Clearly they didn't live in any ranch house. Footbridge women were tough. Who were we? What was I?

We're fakers, ran through my head, middle-class, eastern-educated pretenders. They are the real revolutionaries. This is embarrassing. What should I do? There was no choice. I held my head up high and greeted our guests, hoping that graciousness and good cooking would translate into peace and love, my kind of hippie. It was the start of our larger community of friends.

# CHAPTER 6  Who's Making Love

JUST AS RESTRICTIONS ABOUT CLOTHING AND our bodies dropped away, so did the rules for what we did with those bodies. It was the night of the summer solstice party, quiet after the departure of our guests, black except for the radiance of the moon. Hak and I were nestled in our tree house aerie, content after a day of festivities. Everything was still except for the soft rustle of plants and animals, large and small, going about their nocturnal tasks. We lay high in the branches, peaceful under the dark canopy, knowing that our friends, a few dozen trees away in every direction, shared this space, all of us falling asleep under the same roofless sky to the same muted sounds. Bit by bit the murmur of the night shifted and from across the pasture, deep in the garden, a specific beat came into focus—rhythmic, driving, and familiar. Hak and I cocked our ears and turned to each other knowingly. It was clear from the sounds of lovemaking, somewhat softened by the distance, that Guy and Fairchild were marking the equinox with their own semi-private fertility rites. We scooted closer to each other and I snuggled in, feeling safe with my man by my side. Hak responded and we celebrated along with Guy and Fairchild, us in the heavens, them consecrating the earth.

Guy's attraction to Fairchild waned with the moon, slowly shifting toward the light that Lisa radiated, a liaison much more serious and significantly more complex. Both Guy and Lisa had partners. The goal was not to jettison them but to maintain strong and intimate bonds within each couple while forming a new one in the middle, a seeming contradiction of realities. This was not an easy prospect and it required a lot of thought on everyone's part; theirs to struggle for balance, ours to monitor the play by play. How were they going to work this one out? Happy lovers could be seen hand in hand or head to head enjoying the day together, but the question always remained, "Just who was the duo du jour?" One day it was Guy and Lisa, the next Lisa and Gerald, or perhaps Guy and Janet. Sometimes all four could be seen together. Keeping track was hard, keeping score impossible, even at times for the participants. Sightings of Guy and Gerald walking and talking, gamely trying to build bridges, were duly noted. Everyone was cool, but it was clear there were a lot of hot spots.

Snippets of intense discussions wafted by, the words not explicit but the expressions all too clear.

I tried to stretch my thinking around this new way of loving, but the reach was too far and my mind kept snapping back to the same question. How can they do this? Guy, Lisa, Gerald, and Janet were very earnestly trying to share a relationship. I could go with their flow, but I was clear, there was no possibility that I wanted anything but a traditional monogamous marriage. Having Lev in the picture, a friend, not even a lover, had been too threatening for me. If others wanted to share that was fine. I felt confident that Hak and I were in agreement on this. We had already faced down this particular challenge. There was no doubt in my mind that I needed my man. The ground had fallen out from under me once. Who knew if it would happen again?

In reality we were all in complex relationships, the line between group and couple blurred in the closeness of everyday living. I may not have been sleeping with anyone else and assumed Hakim wasn't either, but intimacy is much more than sex. We did eat, cook, shop, work, bathe, and get high with each other. Every night came to a close around the family dinner table, domestically passing tidbits of food and daily news. When I lovingly prepared meals, it was not just for my husband but for everyone else in the group and they in turn, men and women alike, cooked for me, truly a joyous liberation. What Hak and I could not give each other we found in abundance around us. I was not concerned. After all, wasn't that what we were here for, group living, something bigger than the confines of a couple? Innocently, I believed that if we were sexually exclusive, sharing a bed only with each other, then we were a partnership, a union within the larger picture. I forgot, or never really knew about, the tender mercies and hard-headed battles that over time forge true intimacy. Hakim and I didn't repair the holes between us because we couldn't see them. Every fissure, hurt, and disappointment was formless, lurking under the horizon line of awareness, felt but not named. We didn't talk because we didn't have the words. Instead we sought solace elsewhere. The farm made it easy. If I felt a bump, someone else was always available to pave it over with a friendly ear or warm companionship. Ironically, Guy and Janet spent more time cementing their diluted relationship than Hak and I did on our established marriage.

While Guy and Janet explored sharing partners, gender roles were also changing. Not too far from us lived another collective, the Pageant Players, a guerilla theatre group from New York. We decided to visit them at their rented house, set on a heavily wooded lot, lacking in any charm except for its setting. They welcomed us into the living room, lit on this overcast day by a single exposed bulb that dangled from a wire, fifty bleak watts of power further depressing the ambiance. The only piece of furniture was a frayed and dirty mattress resting directly on the floor. A worn Indian bed spread, slightly askew, partially covered the ticking underneath. The times demanded that we transcend value judgments regarding aesthetics, even as we sought out the beauty of the countryside for its spiritual and healing qualities. I knew the drill and complied, putting away my distaste. Their spirit, not their décor, was what counted.

The group was full of vitality and good cheer, excited over the baby born a few days earlier on the very mattress where I now sat. Both parents proudly showed us their newborn and then retreated, leaving us with the rest of the group. Martine, sitting next to me, struck up a conversation. She cut to substance pretty fast.

"Our goal is to eradicate all traditional gender roles, not just in chores but in bed," she stated. "I mean, have you ever thought about it? Why do women have sex only when men want it?"

I nodded politely and said nothing. My job was to listen and agree.

Martine went on. "I told Ezra that we needed a new plan. We can only sleep together if I take the initiative. He can say no, but that's all. If I don't ask, we don't fuck." Martine's confident dark eyes looked straight into mine, waiting for a response.

"Wow." I replied, offering up my most attentive affect while I mentally scrambled for surer footing. *Take the initiative?* I thought. Wait a minute. I grew up with Cinderella, little singing bluebirds and pink pretty bows. We gave signals, men picked up on them. Only sluts came on heavy. But good girls could enjoy sex. We were, after all, sophisticated and liberated. And what about the mechanics? Men are the ones that have to get it up. We can always fake it. I guess Ezra could tell her no if he wasn't interested. Yeah, right. What guy was never interested?

Martine, sister to sister, continued to wait. I responded to her in a tone that was more heartfelt than I anticipated. "How wonderful that you and Ezra can talk together and work this out." She smiled, pleased, as well she should have been.

# CHAPTER 7   Maggie's Farm

THE TRUTH OF THE ADAGE "wherever you go, there you are" became very clear to me as the days passed. Action had always given my life focus, keeping the demons at bay. Lying around stoned had no appeal for me. I liked achieving things. So here we were, in the Garden of Eden. What do you do in paradise? Me, I produced.

A garden, that's what we needed, fresh vegetables from our own fields. Wasn't that why we were here? In New Haven, I had tended a window full of tiny plants, clucking over them daily, captivated by their ability to grow, each one so different from the other. Now, instead of ten terra-cotta pots stacked on a brick staging area, I had half an acre at hand. I knew nothing, but that was the thrill. Now it was time to jump in. My bible was a mud-stained, water-warped copy of the Rodale Encyclopedia of Organic Gardening, miraculously found at a local secondhand store, one of the first books on the topic. Perched in my tree house, I read it over and over, along with several seed catalogues, referring back and forth between pages, intently scribbling annotations. Seed catalogues are to gardeners what *Playboy* is to men, fertile ground for massaging fantasy. Alone, for hours, I imagined loamy beds of rich dark soil alternating with neat rows of leafy green plants, each one offering up its fruit to be kissed by the sun and plucked by our fingers. There were pendulous eggplants, crispy cucumbers, and voluptuous tomatoes. I never studied a text in graduate school as carefully as I did that book.

Tomatoes were my favorite. Should we have the luscious Big Boys on page six of the full color, illustrated Burpee catalogue, or the smaller Romas that are good for canning? Maybe both—we did want to put food up for the winter. This was thirty years before the emerging food revolution brought epicurean tastings of heirloom produce to local farmers markets. Tomatoes didn't have names. They just had a spot in the produce aisle. Now I had choices. I marked both varieties and double-checked for growth season, sun hours, and zonal classification. Then I turned the page and was face to face with Good Girls, promoted as being resistant to fusarium wilt. That sent me back to Rodale, scanning through the index, looking for plant diseases and bugs. Rodale left no doubt, pesticides were out, natural was in. True believers could achieve miracles through companion planting and by enriching the soil with organic nutrients. There was no need to spray poisons. I could prevent white fly infestation by growing marigolds next to my tomatoes. I was hooked.

Finally, after intensive research, I emerged with my master plan—"The Garden"—a work in half-acre by Margaret Grundstein. But I knew it was not mine alone. We lived together and shared everything. All of us would have to agree. I wrote up my scheme, complete with a diagram for review. Please sign off on this, I penned across the top of the design, and drew little boxes to the right with names by them: Don, Mary Ellen, Clint, Hak, Roggie, Carol, Janet, Fairchild, Rocky, Guy, Lev, and Brandi. Hak's approval and review just part of the group process.

No corporate lackey could have been more organized in passing around an inter-office memo. The plan was circulated and returned to me, but with some unexpected notations. Carol, ever irreverent, always had my number. Eschewing the designated box she scrawled her response, large and bold, in the upper right hand corner: "A+," it read. I got it. Carol had instantly reduced the garden plan to my continuing quest for achievement. There is nothing like living in an intimate group to get a humbling and multifaceted reflection of oneself.

Before we could plant, we needed to till the soil, first plowing and then harrowing to break the dirt into ever smaller particles. I turned to the men for help. We had an old tractor, left in the barn by the landlord, which looked more like a relic for a farm museum than a useful piece of machinery. Clint, a mechanical alchemist who could turn dross into gold, was excited; one person's trash was another person's treasure. He got it to run, although using it was often a stop, tweak, and go situation. Today the goal was to smooth the roughly plowed garden by dragging a heavy log attached to the back of the tractor over the soil, our jerry-rigged alternative to a harrow. We needed to break down the clods. Roggie and Don volunteered for the job, happy to help, high on something other than a strong work ethic. They started the morning at 10:00, each ingesting a tab of acid.

Getting the tractor fired up and out of the barn was the first challenge. Don fiddled with the carburetor and adjusted screws while Roggie worked the clutch and starter. Success! Then they needed to position the makeshift harrow. Roggie and Don struggled to carry the log from the barn to the field. There, they wrapped chains around each end and secured them

*Plowing Greenleaf*

tightly, making sure each was of equal length. Finally, they positioned the log and attached the chains, making sure it was properly lined up behind the tractor. If the pull was uneven, the tractor dragged the log at an angle and it was useless. This set-up could take at least a half an hour, sometimes longer, the variables being the truculence of the log and the whim of the engine.

On this day Don stepped up on the tractor and settled his bottom into the open palm of the metal seat. He started the motor, pleased with the regular firing of the engine. It promised a strong and steady pull. Behind him Roggie squatted low, facing the recalcitrant log, riding shotgun against the dangers inherent in the setup. Everything was in place. They formed a frieze, silhouetted against the sun, awaiting Don's pull at the lever that would set it all in motion. Then the acid hit. Don's last coherent act was to disengage the clutch and shut off the temperamental engine. Roggie looked around. His eye caught every mutating detail. Nothing needed to be said. Together they stepped down, away from the tractor and into another reality, their work for the day done.

Clearly we needed additional help. A young couple, Richard and Helen, along with their new baby Alice, shared our valley. We often saw them plowing their fields, straddling the seat of their new tractor, working hard on their homestead. I asked Mary Ellen and Janet to come with me. Maybe we women couldn't plow, but we certainly knew how to ask for assistance. Our neighbors greeted us cordially. Richard listened carefully, smiled warmly, and said, "Sure, we'd love to plow. We'll come over as soon as we finish up here." Thrilled with our ingenuity, Janet, Mary Ellen, and I walked home and awaited their arrival. Soon their tractor lumbered up our road, slowly coming into focus as it moved closer to our farm.

"Here they come! I can see them."

"Is that Richard driving?"

"I don't know. It doesn't look like him."

"Oh my god, I think it's Helen. Helen's driving."

"You mean that's her on the tractor?"

"Yes, yes. It's Helen."

"Is *she* going to plow?"

We clustered at the edge of our field, a flock of sparrows, all atwitter over what was happening. A woman was driving! A nursing mother with a tiny baby at home whose husband was willing to care for their newborn while she drove off in the tractor. Our men wouldn't stay home to change diapers while we plowed. Then again, we didn't know how to plow.

Just a year ago, I had been working in New Haven, debating if I could get away with wearing pants rather than a skirt to work. "Should I ask my boss if it is okay to wear slacks?" I queried myself. "Nope," was the reply. "Never ask because they might say no. Just do it." And now, putt, putt-ing up the road to our field was a woman who was definitely wearing pants to work. We watched, transfixed. I ran to get my camera and photograph her, our new hero, a woman with milk in her tits and a shaft in her hand, negotiating gears from her perch high on the open tractor, heading forward, but looking back over her shoulder, making sure that the tiller she pulled behind her was raised high enough to avoid the rocks and bumps in the unpaved road between our farms. We waved as Helen passed, running to catch up with her at our field, old ways plowed under as she turned our soil, her husband home rocking their baby to sleep.

I planted a lesser version than my original plan, but that garden, my first, was as beautiful to me as any child is to its mother. Watching the seeds sprout, monitoring their growth, and daily nursing each little bud into fruition was a labor of love. Helen had her baby, the Pageant Players had theirs, and I had mine. Beets sprouted and pushed up from the dark soil, first showing their tufted greens and then their dusky shoulders. Beans ran rampant above ground, their little white flowers giving birth to thin green threads that turned, overnight, into full-fledged haricot verts, ready for dinner, if they made it that far.

None of us had gardened before, let alone tasted fresh produce direct from the ground. We were city kids. Vegetables were still afterthoughts, extras that graced the meat and potatoes of a meal. Salad meant hard round heads of iceberg lettuce. The food revolution arrived on our backs as we discovered the glories of the harvest. Now there was a whole new lexicon of leaf lettuces to explore. I planted butter, Bibb, oak leaf, and black-seeded simpson. If we only harvested the outer leaves, and not the entire head, they would continue to form delicate new growth from their centers, virtual Energizer bunnies of the salad world that kept us in greens for weeks. Pagan religions and fertility goddesses were starting to make sense. Eating a carrot, pulled fresh and warm from the ground, was a ritual as meaningful as a first communion or a bar mitzvah. We crossed a threshold, changed, and committed ourselves to our new truth. Back to nature was one of the things that worked as advertised.

But where were the men? What did those guys do all day? The answer was dope. Wherever and however they could. That was what they planted in *their* garden. Clint, Don, Guy, and Hakim labored under the hot summer sun, wending their way through scratchy undergrowth to hidden plots tucked away in natural clearings. Every drop of water, roll of fencing, and load of fertilizer had to be hand-carried on unmarked paths, a daily chore that required the passion of the converted and the tenacity of an addict. Like womenfolk trading child-rearing techniques, the men were a community unto themselves, full of tales and helpful hints regarding their crops. I watched from the kitchen as they sat outside, passing a joint and slapping their knees, sharing the progress of their homegrown weed. They could have been farmers from a century ago, sitting on cracker barrels in the local general store.

"How's it growin'?"

"Almost up to my chin."

"Nah."

"Yup."

"Must be that manure tea."

"Could be those seeds Johnny gave me."

"Deer eatin' yours?"

"Got one of my best plants."

"You kiddin'?"

"Nope. Gone."

"Glad I put in a fence."

"I'll have to make me one."

These were the keepers of the counterculture, the nurturers of its mainstay. I took care of the vegetables. They took care of the drugs. It was a bumper year.

# CHAPTER 8  Do the Funky Chicken

OUR DREAM WAS SELF-SUFFICIENCY and it seemed quite possible within the fecund richness of western Oregon. Lush blackberries grew along the road, free for the picking, unless of course they had been sprayed by the county to control their growth, the outside world having a way of insinuating its presence. The Pacific Ocean was bountiful, offering up salmon, snapper, and mussels. The creek gave us crayfish. Orchards full of pears, peaches, and apples there for the u-picking. We ate them fresh from the branch, juice dripping down our arms, a sensual delight, awaking us to the full glory of their flavor. We needed a way to store all this natural affluence.

"I've got a freezer. You can have it for $200," said Woody, our neighbor to the north. He lived with his wife, Ruth, in a small cabin on the third homestead in our valley. She helped augment their income by picking pinecones in the woods. Dealers bought the cones by the sack, harvesting the pine nuts inside, a delicacy for humans as well as squirrels. Ruth's efforts seemed well suited to our circumstances: natural, no office, and no commute. I decided to try, joining her as she scavenged the forest floor. The downside rapidly became clear; it was a hard way to earn a living. Trekking through the woods, dragging a gunnysack behind me while I scanned for pine cones grew tiresome. Competing with squirrels was disheartening. I felt like a primitive hunter-gatherer without the panache or mystique of tribal lore. We were two women, dressed in shapeless clothing, moving cone by cone, hour by hour, deeper into poverty. No future here.

Instead, Rocky, Mary Ellen, and I decided to become day laborers and headed off to pick berries. It was stoop labor: hard, hot, and backbreaking. The strawberry fields, as well as the day, went on forever. You had to be fast and even then the paycheck was small. Picking was a skill. By the second day I was getting more efficient, but nowhere near as adept as the brown-skinned professionals next to me. Farm workers of the world unite. I understood. After two days we decided we had enough berries and quit.

Gradually our new freezer filled up with food of all kinds. Friends stopped by with bear and venison. We bought snapper off the boat for twenty-five cents a pound, salmon for just under a dollar. Everything was tightly wrapped and loosely dumped into our nineteen-cubic-foot, cryogenic, second-hand Sear's sarcophagus. When Fairchild gave birth and due to complications was unable to plant her placenta under the big cherry tree in our yard, it too was frozen.

What went in came out. Members of Three Rivers, Footbridge, and our group often visited each other. We all knew that arriving empty-handed was politically incorrect. Our way of life was sharing. If you arrived for a week we fed you for a week. The unspoken agreement was that everyone gave and everyone received. Guests often worked in the garden, helped build a shed, or brought freshly made goat cheese to share with dinner. Food was easy. Western Oregon and the US government were bountiful. We were as good as church ladies, but instead of Jell-O we brought wild greens foraged from beside our creek, garden veggies topped with USDA surplus cheese, or bear meat given to us by a local who wanted an excuse to check us out.

Carol and Clint liked to explore on his motorcycle, looking for land and adventure, mentally mapping old logging roads, abandoned cabins, and far out friends. This day they were headed for Footbridge. Clint went out to rev up his Harley, gunning it to motivate Carol, who was running around trying to find her helmet. "Wait, wait," she called out, buckling her chin strap. "I found my helmet, but we need to bring something."

Carol lifted the lid of our freezer and bent her protected head down into the cold box. She scuffled through hard brown wrapped packages, checking to see if there was any notation that would give a hint as to what was within. Next to two small parcels marked bear meat was a larger one unlabeled. Carol took a quick check. Everything seemed okay; reddish brown, definitely animal, frozen hard, must be bear. Carol grabbed the package, leveled out the remaining packets of frozen food, and shut the freezer lid. "I'm coming, I'm coming," she called over the noise of the motorcycle, heading for the door toward Clint.

After a meandering drive they arrived at Footbridge in the late afternoon. Tchanan was firing up their woodstove in anticipation of dinner, and Johnny had just finished herding their goats back to the shed. Guests made everyone festive. Carol gave Johnny a big hug and offered him the package. "It's bear," she announced with pride and a bit of titillation, always aware of the drama in a scene. Johnny brushed his hands on his pants and received the gift. "Thanks. It'll be a nice change from goat." Tchanan moved to the rough boards that made a work area, ready to prep onions for the fresh meat. Letting the package rest in one hand, Johnny peeled back the brown paper wrapping. Once open, he looked at the defrosted mass and then leaned in and peered closer. Quizzically, Johnny poked at the meat with his rough forefinger. Instead of resisting, it jiggled. For all his rural acumen, Johnny was a man of the world, with a great sense of the dramatic himself. He looked up at Carol and then at Clint. "This," he said, dangling the flesh from his fingers for everyone to see, "is a placenta!" And so it was. Everyone laughed, even Carol, who was used to her own foibles. Tchanan moved back to boiling beans while Carol set out wooden bowls on the rough table for supper.

Although some new mothers espoused eating a small bit of the placenta after their baby was born, this particular afterbirth was not devoured either that night or at a later date. As a matter of fact its whereabouts seemed a bit murky after that visit. Luckily, Fairchild never asked.

We lived in the present, without any concern for future income, trusting that our needs would be met, and they were. One benefactor was the United States Department of Agriculture. We signed up for their food surplus program, qualified, and got five-pound bricks of cheese, gallon tins of peanut butter, and bags of rolled oats. There was little moral quandary in receiving these items. They were surplus, extra, part of the mismanaged bounty of our land. We weren't taking money, just foodstuff that would rot if we didn't, a win-win situation, although getting something for nothing did feel a bit compromising.

In 1971 Congress replaced the surplus program with food stamps, requiring that allotments be equivalent to the cost of a nutritionally adequate diet. How thoughtful. This was definitely a windfall. We were nothing if not poor, of our own choosing of course, collateral damage from our higher calling. Food stamp coupons looked like monopoly dollars, each denomination a different color—pink, blue, green, and white—their face value printed boldly in the center, ranging from five to twenty dollars. It was easy to see it all as a game, as long as I did not pull the "Go directly to jail, do not pass go" card. There was no reason to worry. We were legit, fooling only our government, the one that had abandoned reason and run amok.

If this was so, why did I feel self-conscious as I sat in the local office of social services, face to face with my own caseworker? Lying for peanut butter and oatmeal felt very different than faking it for surrogate money. This was one step away from welfare. Below my bravado and rhetoric sat shame. Cheater is always an epithet, never a badge of honor. My fall from grace, out of the cocoon of middle-class respectability, was hard to swallow. I identified with the economic strata that gave away money, not the population that received it. Shopping at the grocery store became stressful. At the check-out counter, I would hold the coupon books in the palm of my hand, down by the side of my leg, while the checker rang up my purchases. When it came time to tear out the correct amount I would hunch my shoulders, trying to keep any prying eyes from seeing that I wasn't using real money. My goal was to pay and leave, fleeing discomfort as fast as I could. I knew the figure I cut did not sit well with many of the working families behind me. Long hair, scruffy clothes, food stamps; I was an alien, a stereotype, a free loader. If there were two or more of us in the check-out line, it helped. We created our own emotional climate, deflecting any chill winds that might be blowing. Working and paying my share, even perhaps a little more, was my ethic. When I applied for food stamps that line was crossed, and like most lines, once crossed it tended to fade. Government largesse became a way of life, augmenting our other sources of income and food.

We wanted to be self-sufficient. Protein was always the challenge. Meat and eggs came from animals with hearts that beat and eyes that could see. They were alive, just like us, although we were starting to feel that even lettuces had an aura.

Our farm came with chickens. They were housed in a coop with a small fenced yard. This in itself created a dilemma. How could we confine them when we so fully understood the need to be unfettered? Should chickens have free will? We debated this over many dinners at our communal table, our final decision being no decision. Living without a leader, too many egos for anyone to be a follower, meant inaction became our action. What we could agree upon was that we needed to expand our flock. Driven by artistic and dramatic sensibilities, our choices were more aesthetic than practical. Araucana chickens laid blue and pink eggs. How could we pass on that? Polish Crested, with tufted feathers at the top of their heads, looked like Albert Einstein. We were captivated. This was the fun part—shopping, designing our collection of birds and eggs. Caring for the chickens, however, was another matter. Animal husbandry was drudgery. Shoveling chicken shit was nobody's idea of fun, and if it wasn't fun it tended not to get done. Only the local weasel seemed interested in doing any cleaning and his efforts, directed at the flock, not their roost, were at cross purposes with ours.

As with the garden, harvesting eggs was a sacrament. The days were lengthening. Our hens were laying. We didn't need to shop. We could provide for ourselves. Guy and Janet were making zucchini bread with squash harvested from our garden. Zucchini, like radishes, were a gift to every new gardener, massaging fragile egos with their ease and abundance. Every group was always on the giving and receiving end of excess summer squash. Today, ours were going into a sweet treat. "Could you get us some eggs?" Guy called out to me. "Sure," I replied, heading out the kitchen door while Janet rotated the handle on the grinder, turning wheat berries from our fifty-pound bag into flour. I was excited. Collecting eggs expanded our consciousness in ways that drugs promised but couldn't deliver. The miracle of reaching under the warm body of our live chickens and pulling out breakfast was seductive. This was real organic shopping. I walked out to the coop, alert and a little anxious. To the side of the small shed was a messy heap of straw and chicken droppings, a monument to our ability to start something and then leave it unfinished. Someone had cleaned the coop, but never disposed of the mess. We had great plans for composting but were not organized about realizing them. Skirting the pile, I held my breath to avoid the stench and reached for the piece of wood that served as a latch. The chicken coop was dusky inside with strips of sunshine filtering through the cracks in the walls. Dust motes floated in the shaft of light coming from the open door. Six hens sat on their nests. Each and every shiny chicken eye was on me. I looked at them, they looked at me, a momentary stand-off. He not being born is busy dying, I thought, not quite remembering the words to Bob Dylan's refrain. "The best defense is a good offense" also rambled around in there. It was time to gather the eggs. Actually pillage seemed a more accurate verb. I selected my bird, and with my head slightly averted out of guilt and squeamishness, moved carefully toward her. Wary of being pecked, I slowly stretched out my hand and then I did it. I touched her breast. It was warm and surprisingly soft. Now I had to move down and under, a little more intimate, and steal her unborn offspring. I felt like a marauding conqueror, while simultaneously identifying with the hen in our sisterhood. Grab it, get out, and hope that there is nothing slimy on it. I turned my head away, did the deed and left, one warm egg in the palm of my hand. Ecstatic, I ran back to the kitchen, the feel and smell of the chicken still with me. I was connected to the source of food, of life, of the bond between animals and humans, of survival. Preschoolers see chickens and eggs in their earliest picture books. It seems commonplace. But that day, reaching in under the warm, dusty body of the wary chicken and pulling out an egg, I expanded and clearly knew it was far beyond where parsing zoning regulations would have taken me.

Our next philosophical dilemma was the chickens themselves. If we were going to eat them, not only their eggs, we needed to kill them. I was just discovering the miracle of life and now we were to be the harbingers of death. Providing food was becoming an emotionally fraught experience, but a principle was at stake. We needed to be in touch with the process of putting food on the table, one of the primal aspects of life. Participating in this sacrament became a rite of passage, all very logical, but how do you do it? None of us had killed an animal. The time had come. Our obvious choice was the chickens, the older ones. We had goats, but we needed their milk, actually more an excuse than a reason. Goats, like us, were large mammals, and that made them a little too close on the classification scale for comfort.

If we wanted a chicken dinner, the recipe was clear. First we had to chop off their heads. Next we had to pluck their feathers and then eviscerate them. These terms were a little harsher than the usual mix, fold, and blend. Plucking didn't seem too bad, just messy, but eviscerate was another matter. Was I supposed to reach in and grab the warm, slippery entrails in my fingers and then disembowel my dinner? I put that thought aside and moved on to the first order of business.

The dilemma was how to get a chicken to lie down and put its head out long enough for us to lower the axe. Hakim and Rocky worked out a scheme where they put a noose around the head of a chicken and stretched its neck over our chopping block, a sawed-off round of wood. Rocky held the chicken. Hakim, as executioner, beheaded the bird, taking care not to render the same fate to his accomplice.

If they could do it, so could we. Carol and I had a need to justify ourselves out here in man's country. We, too, wanted to feel righteous about providing food. Hak and I did not share the slaughter. No, that was something he did with another man, and there were plenty to choose from living in a group. Carol and I turned to each other, both of us full of trepidation. If I thought getting an egg was a challenge, I knew that murdering the mother of that egg was an even bigger one.

First we had to catch the hen that was squawking in distress and fluttering about, alternating escape and attack strategies. We were just as nervous as the chicken and equally as flighty, chasing it down and then covering our heads when it dove toward us. Carol and I isolated one near the coop. She made a fast grab and was successful. Winded, but proudly victorious, Carol wrapped her arms around the bird, clutching it to her body to keep it still and buy time for the next step. I held the rope we prepared and slipped the noose over the chicken's neck, letting the loose end dangle to the ground. There was no escaping it. Now we had to kill the thing. Which was worse, holding the warm live body of the chicken, keeping it still and fighting off its efforts to escape, or actually doing the deed? Neither looked too good. My mind briefly flashed with the image of a biblical custom our Jewish ancestors had practiced known as Kapparot. I could see a wizened Jewish bubbe in Poland, maybe even my own great grandmother, complete with babushka and bandy legs, swinging a live chicken in a circle above the bent head of her child. With each of the three circles a prayer is spoken, offering the fowl as an exchange in place of the supplicant. The hope is that the bird, which is then donated to the poor for food, will take on any misfortune that might otherwise occur to the child. This idea briefly caught my fancy.

"Hey, Carol. What about that thing where they sling the chicken around three times. Should we try that?" We were hooked on Indian lore and tribal myths, why not some kind of ritual from our own tribe, even if it was a little less classy. Pagan myths from more macho cultures seemed to hold more sway.

Carol looked up at me, over the humped body of our victim, its head struggling under her arm. "Your sins or mine, Margaret?"

Actually she was right on target. I wanted this particular chicken to absorb my sins, most specifically my role as its agent of death. All in all, a lot to ask of the condemned.

A few more squawks brought me back to the task at hand. Time to make a choice. I'll do anything, I thought, as long as I don't have to hug that warm struggling bird against my breast, to feel our bond and be reminded that it is a living, breathing creature doing its best, just like me, to walk through life on this earth.

"I don't want to touch it. You hold it and I'll do the axe," I told Carol and walked over to where it lay on the ground.

"OK," she agreed, "but how do I pull on the rope and stretch out its body at the same time?"

"I don't know." I was feeling a little less confident. "Maybe we should put another rope around its legs so you can pull from both ends?"

"This thing won't keep still," Carol noted as the chicken escaped in a flutter of wings and shrill clucking. We chased it down again, laughing, covering our heads when it dove toward us once more.

"I got it!" Carol called out, the chicken caught once again in her embrace. She approached the death stump.

"I don't want to see any blood or loose chicken heads hanging around. I wish I could just close my eyes," I told her.

"Hurry up!" Carol screamed as the bird jerked against her restraints. "And make sure you don't get me instead of the chicken." We hadn't quite figured that part out yet.

"Lean back and to the side and you should be safe." I picked up the axe, stepped off the right distance and then put it down again. "What if I miss and just hurt it?"

"Just do it!" was Carol's muffled reply, her head down and facing away, as far from the kill zone as she could get it.

Whomp! The axe fell as did the head of the chicken. We succeeded, but it was bitter fruit. Food stamps looked better and better each day.

Like any traditional family, eating together anchored us as a group, the dining room our communal nexus. Set between the kitchen and the living room, it was both the true and magnetic center of our home. A rough-hewn picnic table made of weathered planks ran the length of the dining room, leaving just enough space for two long benches on either side and shorter ones at the ends. Dinner became the unifying ritual as the day ended and we headed toward the heart of the house. We were like cattle at dusk, randomly gathering from all corners of the field, no call or reminder needed. Tonight was special. It was Clint's thirty-fourth birthday. Outside, the evening light faded. Inside, Roggie strode along the tabletop in his boots, wielding a broom, sweeping away the detritus of the previous meal. I chose to ignore my concerns about hygiene and focused instead on appreciating his ingenuity. Ours was a "live and let live" life. There was no room at the table for the uptight.

I sat next to Hakim with Gerald and Lisa down the bench from me. Kerosene lanterns lit the room, giving off a soft light. We had deliberately moved out of the present and back to a simpler time. One look around the table made this clear. None of the women wore make-up or stylish clothes. Instead, our hair, worn loose and free, was our only adornment. No embellishment was needed. We grew our own. The men mirrored us with manes that fell to their shoulders and beards that bushed out several inches from their faces, leaving cheeks, eyes, and lips as islands in a hirsute sea. All of us looked like illustrations from *Little House on the Prairie*, glowing, in the gentle warmth of our kerosene lanterns, from the light of good health and camaraderie. We were every *Saturday Evening Post* cover, every Hallmark card sentiment, and every myth of the American frontier, just fuzzier around the edges and funkier in our wearing of the diadem. How could the world not love us? We were their dream come true.

"Did you know that the fork was first used in the Middle Ages?" asked Roggie, casting out into the conversation that flowed around him. "I was reading the current issue of *Gourmet* and they had an article on the history of the fork."

Roggie's factual tidbit piqued my interest. Really, forks have a history? I wonder why they date back to that time. Then suddenly, my mind flipped to another dimension and the contradictions around me came into full relief. Here we were, minimally groomed and roughly clothed, looking not too different from the original users of the fork, still receiving my forwarded five-year subscription to *Gourmet* magazine while we dined by the grace of government subsidies and garden greens.

"Forks, mostly being two-tined, were known as 'split spoons,'" Roggie continued. "Although there are examples of four- and five-tined forks from before the 1600s, the four-tined fork became popular only in the late 1800s." His hungry mind looked for knowledge wherever he could find it.

"Well, I don't know about those guys in the Middle Ages, but we sure seem to have a few two-tined forks of our own," Guy interjected in his slow Texas drawl, sporting a mischievous grin and holding up a twisted specimen salvaged from our utensil drawer.

Lisa's soft voice broke in, "Whatever fork you have, make sure you save it for Clint's birthday cake." She lifted her long white dress, stepped over the bench, and went into the kitchen, returning with a confection she had baked earlier in the day, a hearty cake made with hand-ground, whole wheat flour and topped with a carob glaze. Lisa set her offering down in the middle of the table. "This is a magic cake," she said, extending her spell of gentleness and love. "Before putting it in the oven, I put my ring in the batter. Whoever gets the ring will be blessed with good luck."

Lisa cut through the layers and graciously served us each a piece. Chatter started up again as everyone devoured the treat, complimenting Lisa on how good it was, hoping for more. Abruptly, Clint's voice shot through the babble of conversation, his hand reaching up to his jaw, his face perplexed. "My tooth! I think I broke my tooth."

Everyone watched as Clint ran his tongue around his mouth, finding the molar that was indeed chipped. He spat into his hand and looked up, smiling. Sitting in his fingers was Lisa's ring, the birthday talisman, for everyone to see. Next to it was a tiny piece of enamel.

"I'm sorry." Lisa murmured, embarrassed and concerned.

"Hey Clint, glad you got the good luck and not me."

"Say Clint, you're getting old enough for false teeth anyway."

Laughter, commiseration, apologies, and jokes abounded. We were a group, all of us together at the table, dinner a time to feed ourselves in so many ways.

# CHAPTER 9   Sweet Baby James

THE PAGEANT PLAYERS HAD THEIR NEW BABY. It was time for ours. Fairchild was pregnant. The working assumption of everyone, including Guy, was that the child was his. It didn't matter. We welcomed this new life that would make us complete as a family. Fairchild, pregnant, was the perfect accessory for our collective vision, very conveniently giving birth for us. She was Christ in reverse. We were all grateful for her gift, especially those of us with wombs. Certainly none of us overeducated women were going to tie our independent selves down to an infant. Maybe later, but right now we had other adventures to pursue.

Fairchild's pregnancy went easily, as was her nature. In retrospect, her lack of prenatal care seems appalling. She had none. For her delivery she chose a home birth, assisted by a midwife, an African American man with limited training and an affordable fee. As a precaution he did require that she use a house in Eugene that was at least closer to a hospital than our farm. Fairchild's choice was risky. Midwives, even those with more training, were illegal in or out of a hospital and if complications arose, there was no back-up from the medical system. When labor started Guy drove Fairchild into town. Brandi joined them as the birth coach and at Fairchild's request I came along to photograph. I loved documenting the excitement and whimsy of our lives. Don's dad let me develop and print my black and white film in his darkroom.

I knew that Fairchild's delivery was momentous both as a political statement and as a timeless miracle. The crowning of a tiny head out of her body and into this world was an adventure I was not going to miss even if it did make me squeamish. The thought of watching Fairchild's vulva stretch and distend, possibly even tear, made me uneasy—a little too intimate and a lot too visceral. I had never looked between the spread legs of another woman before. Determined to move past these obstacles, I hefted my camera, focused my lens, and shot everything from the first antiseptic wash to the sweet, sweet suckling at the end.

We were all new at this and blithely innocent of the risks involved. Birth was a natural process. Having the baby at home, then saving the placenta to plant deep under the roots of our massive cherry tree, bound us to the juicy primordial ooze of womanhood. Or so I thought. In truth I was ignorant, able to drift with Fairchild because it wasn't my body and it wasn't my baby. We were lucky. Everything went well and Fairchild returned to the farm, her daughter Shine tucked in her arms, the afterbirth deep in her bag.

We gave Fairchild the downstairs bedroom off the dining area, next to the bath. Shine, our first homegrown infant, thrived. Her mother did not. Fairchild started to lose energy and within a week she developed a fever that stayed around 102, sometimes spiking higher. How had things come full circle? Wasn't this what women used to die from? Hakim called an impromptu gathering around the dining room table. I sat across from him and listened intently as he laid out his strategy. Hak, his face serious with concern, jumped to the core of our dilemma, shrewdly preempting debate.

"We can't call a doctor. The delivery was illegal." He looked around at each of us. "She could get arrested," he added, "and the midwife will for sure."

"What are we going to do?" Rocky said, getting nervous. "We're not doctors."

Hakim's face relaxed into confidence. "We have to break the fever. I've done it before." He moved into the plan. "First we need to get the bedroom hot and wrap her body in blankets. Janet, I need you to fill every pot in the house with water and bring it to a full boil. Then," he instructed, "pour the hot water into bowls and place them around her room. I want as much steam as we can get. We have to raise her body temperature." Hak took charge. It was us against the Man; we can do it ourselves. He stood up, stepped over the bench, and entered Fairchild's room. I joined Janet, following her into the kitchen, ready to help in any way I could, secretly thrilled by Hak's willingness to walk where most men feared to tread. Surely this meant he would be a wonderful father and supportive husband when we decided to have our own child, our own little east meets west baby.

The downstairs bedroom with Fairchild and Shine became the focus of our attention, Hakim the dramatic center, the rest of us concerned witnesses. Although there was nothing to see but the closed bedroom door, we could feel, hidden behind it, the heaviness of fear and illness. Only Hakim and people he designated were allowed to enter. I wasn't one of them. From time to time, Hak, sweating, with his sleeves rolled up, would crack open the door and indicate, in a low but intense voice his need for hotter water, more towels, or extra blankets. Guy, the presumptive father, was with him along with Janet. They moved from the inner sanctum to our waiting faces, fetching what was needed, receiving what was requested. Together they worked for hours, sometimes supporting Fairchild as she moved, weak and passive, from her bed to a hot soak in the tub. Outside the sky darkened. Inside we continued our vigil. What was going on? When the door opened, I saw a painting, a still life, lit by candles, diffused by steam, its edges receding into shadow. A mattress sat on the floor in the center of the room; on top was the mounded form of a body: no face, no person, just a shrouded form, still and quiet. Hakim, barefoot, squatted in the corner of the room stirring herbs into a bowl between his feet.

I hovered outside the closed door like everyone else, each of us quietly tense and concerned. What if Fairchild died? And, the baby, Shine, who would take care of her? For that matter, what about us? Questions multiplied and seditious doubts formed, accumulating like forbidden sin. Hak seemed in charge but he looked apprehensive. Did he really know what he was doing? Shouldn't we call someone? Inside myself I heard a voice say, "Screw Hakim. This woman needs a doctor!" But I didn't speak up. Too many egos, all of them male, were at work creating an ethic I felt couldn't be questioned. Hours passed. Hak finally came out of Fairchild's room, exhausted and spent. A few of us were still waiting at the table. "The fever has broken," he announced, as much to himself as to the rest of us. "She's going to be fine." There was a great sense of relief. We believed and trusted. Why? Because our self appointed shaman, my husband, said so. Evidently that was enough, at least for everyone else. Guilt seeped in. What kind of a wife was I?

# CHAPTER 10 Take Good Care of My Baby

WE WERE LUCKY. I KNEW THAT. We had all played with fate. This time Fairchild recovered, but I knew Hak would challenge us to trust and jump again.

Would I follow? Of course, even if it meant struggling with doubt. Hadn't we had shed old ways like dirty clothes? Didn't we awaken each day to dress afresh, inside and out, in the raiment of our new glory? This was home, my old life far behind. Inside, however, was a tiny voice that questioned. Anxiety was a familiar place for me, but something was off. Maybe my qualms were not just fear. Where did we draw the line? I felt mine slowly forming, its place becoming clearer.

As the green of Oregon replaced the darkness of New Haven, I healed. Peace and love, the hippie mantra, sounded trite, but I thrived under its mantle. We were living a life that matched my temperament, harmony instead of combat. I also refused to take any drugs. It didn't matter that everyone else smoked daily and tripped whenever they could. I needed to protect my sanity. Every week that passed without a horrifying hallucination or crippling panic gave me strength, reassuring me that what happened in New Haven was an acid-based anomaly, not something that would be repeated. In this mood of growing confidence, several months after the birth of Shine, I drove to Eugene to use the darkroom.

Don's parents were out of town for a few days, leaving me alone to do my work and water their plants. Rocky, who had driven me into Eugene, stopped by on the second day before heading back to the farm. We sat in the neatly appointed kitchen.

"I picked up a hitchhiker on the way here. She's really nice. I'm bringing her back to the farm."

"Where is she now?" I asked, looking out toward our battered truck.

"She needed to pick up a few things," he replied with a slightly proprietary air. "She has a tiny baby, a little girl."

"Another baby! Wonderful. How long will she be staying?"

"Who knows?" he said, putting his empty mug in the sink, smiling. "But I'd better get going. I told her I'd meet up with her in an hour."

Rocky left and I returned to the darkroom, my thoughts centered on the baby. People came and people went, but an infant—that was exciting. Maybe she'd still be there when I got back.

The next morning I brought in the daily *Oregonian* from the front porch and tossed it on the Whites' kitchen table. It landed headline up. My eyes caught the bold dark print: *Babysitter Kidnaps Infant*. Knowledge hit like a vision, complete and sure. Anxiously I scanned the article. All the details matched. A young couple had hired a girl to watch their infant and the babysitter had disappeared with the baby. I turned on the television. Every channel interrupted their regular bulletins with announcements by the distraught parents begging for their three-month-old little girl. We didn't have TV or newspapers at the farm. No one there would know we were harboring a kidnapper. Full of adrenaline, I called home. Clint picked up.

"You've got a kidnapper," I blurted out, too excited for niceties. "Rocky gave her a ride. That's not her baby. It's all over the news. Everything matches. I'm sure it's the same girl."

Clint was unruffled. He confirmed the hitchhiker was there and said he would check out the situation. I felt relieved, confident the authorities would be notified and the baby returned to her parents. After a bit I rang the farm again.

"What did she say when you told her about the baby?" I asked Clint, who had once again picked up my call.

"Well," he drawled, "we're still working on it."

"You mean nothing's been done?" I barked into the phone. "No one has confronted her?"

Clint explained there was a lot of discussion going on about the right course of action.

"The right course of action," I sputtered, feeling Hakim's influence. I could just hear him. "Don't call the pigs. We can handle it. She'll give us the baby." This was turning into every bad Western we suckled on as children, mixed in with a big scoop of hippie hubris. We don't need no sheriff, this is our land. Out here on the frontier we take care of things ourselves, just like we did with Fairchild.

I had a different perspective standing in the middle-class kitchen, miles from our cut-off little utopia. The newspaper sat in front of me and the TV blared desperate appeals and news updates. I saw the grieving young couple and heard their sobbing pleas. This was a crime. I hung up the phone, shaken. Someone needed to call the police. Would Hakim be furious? Would everyone at the farm hate me? I hesitated, and then reached for the phone.

"Hello, I need to speak with a person about the missing baby and the girl that took her. I think I know where you can find them." The officer on the other end was attentive as I gave him my story. I hung up and quickly dialed again.

"Clint, I've called the police. They're on their way. They should be there in about forty minutes." I wanted everyone at the farm to have a heads up. I was no fool. They needed to hide the dope.

"Okay," Clint said without shock or recrimination. "Thanks. We'll take care of things." What a relief. His response seemed like an affirmation of my decision. Of course it was. This was the right thing to do.

At the farm, negotiations between Hakim and the girl were in progress when the police arrived. In spite of his best efforts, she denied kidnapping the baby and refused to give it up. When the police got there it became a moot point. They took the baby and arrested the girl, leaving an officer to wrap things up. Roggie described the scene to me when I got home.

He, along with Hak, Clint, Guy, and Don, stood in a semicircle opposite the clean-cut young cop, silent, facing off against the symbol of authority. The cop asked questions. Hakim gave terse answers. Trying to be patient, the cop explained that the police were there to help. No response. The alliance was an awkward one for both sides.

"Actually," Roggie told me, "we were quite rude. I felt very bad for him. I'm the son of a cop, and knowing it from the other side made me uncomfortable."

Back in Eugene, as I waited for a ride home, I started to doubt. Fear seeped in. I found myself hoping someone beside my husband would pick me up. Could I stand up to Hakim? Was I really right? I hated facing the blade of his sharp mind when he argued doctrine. He never doubted himself. That was it. Right there is where our frisson happened, where we pressed on each other and the electricity buzzed. Not in bed, which wasn't our hot spot, but in power and control, which inhabit all the rooms of our shared selves. I fought it and sought it. That must have been true for Hak as well; after all, what feeds the passion of a crusader more than the resistance of the unbeliever and the thrill of prevailing. I was blind to the fact that other and better dances were possible. This time was different, though. I had finally challenged him. We had moved off our center.

In the midst of my worry, a vehicle pulled into the driveway. I looked out the window. Hakim sat in the cab of our truck, stone-faced, waiting. I gathered up my things, locked the Whites' front door, and we headed back, stuck in the truck together, just the two of us.

"You never call the pigs! Never! Do you understand that?" Hak jabbed the air with his finger as he drove, emphasizing each angry point. "We take care of things."

I started the ride sitting up, silent, staring forward through the cracked windshield. As he continued, I moved as far away as I could in the cab until I was pressed up against the door. Then I tucked myself in and folded over, laying my head on the seat in the space between us. I shut my eyes and tried to tune Hakim out. All I wanted was to disappear. Please stop, I begged in my mind. I can't stand this. Please, please, just stop.

I was a failure in this noble new cause, clearly not up to the task of change. How could I have called the police? Yet no matter how inadequate I felt, how much he bludgeoned me with moral imperative, I knew, deep inside, where that baby belonged. She needed to be safely in the arms of her parents. Now! That was the only truth.

Even with this knowledge, I continued to berate myself, vacillating under his barrage. Clearly, my heritage, five thousand years of perfecting Jewish guilt, was not wasted on me. I kept up a steady rhythm in my head, an echo of the litany for Yom Kippur where congregants mournfully tap their chest chanting an alphabetic list of their transgressions, atoning in the hope of forgiveness. There I sat, hunched over, silently drowning in my failures. No I am not adventurous. Yes I get anxious. No I am never radical enough. It was one self-flagellation after another, until I got it. Oh yes, I got it! At least I won't have to carry within me, for the rest of my life, the endless unbearable weight of assisting a tragedy. I knew I had done the right thing and I knew with equal certainty that Hakim was never, ever going to back me up on this. I would have to do it for myself. Amen.

For a few months Hak initiated visits to the kidnapper in the mental institution where she was incarcerated. He wanted to be supportive of the young woman. The visits also served another purpose, a silent stand, low key but enduring, for Hakim's belief that he could have solved everything if he had just been given enough time.

I never went, nor did I feel any sympathy for Hakim or the girl.

*Roggie building his boat at Greenleaf*

# CHAPTER 11   Money Honey

MONEY WAS EASY, AT FIRST. A bit of cash, some unemployment checks, and a few lingering tax refunds maintained the flow, bounty from the past that made our present possible. We shared as we saw fit, openly proud of our collective life, quietly protective of our personal needs. There was no plan. We didn't talk about it. Instead, in the low thrum at the threshold of consciousness, we, like the rest of the world, made endless calculations. Who has money, who doesn't, who pays, who can't, what's mine, what isn't—strivings, comparisons, and resentments, so ever-present they were invisible. All this was embedded in us. We brought it along, packed right in with our paisley bedspreads and ten-pound blocks of government surplus cheese. The universal laws of capital still held sway; if you had cash you had say, over your life as well as the lives of others. This was a frontier that begged to be crossed.

Our initial attempts were informal, easing the balance but not tipping it. Roggie needed help. His real destination was Indonesia, not the farm, but we were welcoming and a plane ticket to Southeast Asia cost more than he could muster. After a few months Roggie had an epiphany. If he couldn't fly, he would sail across the Pacific, not on a freighter, not as crew, but in his own, handcrafted, Polynesian-style catamaran. No one questioned the wisdom of this approach. After all, who among us could say the emperor had no clothes? Weren't we all living the impossible dream? Roggie's plan merely reinforced our collective vision right at that delicate spot where idealism flirts with delusion.

As a scholar, his first step was the library, where he researched his topic. Next he cleared out space in the barn and built two pontoon frames raised on sawhorses, elegant pieces of south sea sculpture. The boat was taking shape. Roggie spent hours delicately tap-tap-tapping with a narrow-headed hammer, wrapping the curved hulls in long, elegant strips of wood. This was cedar, cut to fit. Money was involved. Someone was backing Roggie, but who? Nothing had been decided as a group. Instead, unknowingly, we had reverted to an age-old system, patronage, though very loosely applied. A trip to town, stoned musings, and the next thing you know, Hakim was delivering a load of fresh lathing for the skin of the pontoons. Guy helped by providing nautical glue and nails. Bit by unplanned bit, backing appeared, and the boat took form. Not everyone participated. Clint offered technical advice instead of cash, choosing to invest in a lathe for turning bowls instead, a tempting toy that everyone, or at least everyone who was male, got to use.

Things bumbled along in this manner, until the inevitable happened. Hakim, our ideologue in residence, always ready to push a bit further, laid down a challenge. We had driven into town that morning to pick up his unemployment check, the only source of cash for the two of us. Everyone was in the dining room when we returned home, relaxing around the remains of a meal, chatting, and lighting up the obligatory postprandial joint. Fairchild, nursing Shine, scooted over to make room. Hak and I sat down on the rough wood bench and helped ourselves to bowls of brown rice and fresh tomato salad. We bobbed along with the flow, catching up with the group. Guy mentioned the need to buy another fifty-pound sack of wheat berries. With the *Tassajara Bread Book* at their side, he and Janet did most of our baking, and they were running low, a fact that would affect us all.

"Can anyone chip in to help with the cost?" Guy requested reasonably.

"I'm broke," said Rocky, rolling his eyes balefully.

Clint, without saying anything, tossed a few dollars across the table. Then Hakim stood up, silent, waiting. His very stance put him at center stage. While everyone watched, he deliberately reached into the right front pocket of his jeans. His delicate brown fingers emerged with a pile of twenties, neatly folded in half. This was some serious change being brought into the light of day. Cash was in short supply and discretely hidden if you had it. Everyone waited. We knew Hak was up to something. And then, there it was. Hak slammed the money down on the table, his entire unemployment check, the one we had just cashed. He stood erect and looked around.

"What you see is everything we have," he announced, a fact that resonated deep inside me. He moved his hand away and stood tall, waiting. Then Hak played the high card.

"This," he gestured with his head, "is no longer mine. Now it belongs to all of us."

What a move. No one had even been betting and Hak trumped them all. He knew what he was doing. This was more than money, it was a line drawn in the sand, an in-your-face challenge. Who would have the nerve to match him?

I was shocked. That was our money. It belonged to both of us. Just a moment ago I had cash, and now I had nothing. My partner had given away every cent we owned. Inside my head I fumed. Hey Hak, what about ME! Last time I noticed we were married. That money you just slapped down on the table was ours, yours and MINE. You just gave it away without even a thought toward me. Nothing. Not one word. Not even a glance. Where's the 'we' in that move, Hakim? Tell me! Where's the goddamn 'we' in that move? These thoughts fired like flares in my mind.

"Hak?" I said quietly, tentatively trying to get his attention, knowing that this was not the time to initiate a full-out domestic dispute.

There was no response. The drama was elsewhere. Everyone was quiet, waiting. The small pile of bills in front of Hak lay there, a challenge and a reproach. Then it hit me. He was right. This was why we were here. Ownership was the devil we needed to confront. Private property divided. We longed to join. There was no way I would complain or speak out. Questioning my husband or even suggesting that we table this discussion until the two of us consult privately faded in importance. I remained silent along with everyone else, eyes locked on Hakim. High Noon in Hippieville. Clint, across from Hak, slowly reached his rough hand deep into his own Levis, drew out some crumpled bills and added them to the ante. Mano a mano, the face-off was met.

"That's it," Clint said, a note of irritation in his voice. "That's all I am putting in. I'm not giving away all my money."

He was not going to be manipulated by Hakim and find himself at the mercy of the group. Clint, silent and strapping, was a leader, not a follower. He knew the subtle ways of power. At six foot three, Clint, with his long muscular torso and broad capable shoulders, stood tall and strong among men. I had seen him, in the presence of another big man, discreetly step up on a fallen log, retaking the edge, the height that crowned a king. Like Hak he made his own rules and set his own priorities.

There was a short silence and then Roggie broke in.

"I don't have any money so it's a moot point." This loosened the mood. The show was over. Hakim sat down and the conversation picked up, everyone rambling on about money but without any plan coming to the fore. We were too many egos and too unorganized, both by choice and happenstance, to ever have any financial structure.

Later Clint approached me.

"My truck needs new valves and the two front tires are looking worn," he said. "I want some welding tools. There's a big fifty-gallon drum I'd like to turn into a smoker."

I listened sympathetically, understanding his conflict.

"Let Hakim do it if he wants," Clint said. "I'm holding onto my cash."

That made sense to me. I also knew he had to consider Carol. She was back east trying to sublet her apartment. Giving it all up was not her style. Nor was it Clint's. He was an alpha male. He needed to have money, his own money, right there in the pocket of his pants, nestled warmly in the curve of his groin.

Clint may have stood his ground that day, but Hakim spoke to our dreams and played on our emotions, shaking the precepts beneath our feet, setting off subterranean shifts that continued to build pressure. He was, as usual, on the moral high road, leading us out of the thicket of our old life. This very experiment would not have come into existence if we hadn't broken barriers, prodded in part by his charismatic leadership.

"You know, Margaret, Hak is the linchpin of this whole deal," Guy told me one day as we hung out in the kitchen, munching on thick slices of dense whole wheat bread smeared with commodity peanut butter. "He's a big inspiration, so egalitarian, so willing to help anybody."

I nodded, proud of my man, but not quite sure he was the saint Guy made him out to be. Clint, overhearing the conversation, joined us in the kitchen.

"Hakim has a talent. He can get all us crazy people to head in the same direction, at least some of the time, and think we're okay with it. That's his strength. He makes it happen."

If these guys were swayed, what chance did I have?

# CHAPTER 12 Summertime

I PRESSED A WARM BERRY WITH MY TONGUE, mashing the tiny globes against my palate. The juice tasted like sweet perfume. Mary Ellen and I were picking blackberries for dinner, moving from one perfect cluster to the next as we filled our containers, empty commodity peanut butter cans. "Are you eating them all or are you saving some for dessert?" Mary Ellen asked. "Both," I replied, popping another one into my mouth. Mary Ellen looked down at her tin and then glanced over at mine. "This should be more than enough." I nodded in agreement, distracted by six swollen berries that promised to be the sweetest of them all. One by one I pulled at them, feeling each berry separate from its core and fall into the curve of my palm. They were lightly covered with dust and fuzz, still warm from the sun. I slipped them into my mouth and savored the moment as much as the fruit. Sunlight warmed my body, sweet juice ran down my throat, an open day lay ahead, and I had provided for my own. There was nothing else to want.

"Could you take them back?" I asked, knowing Guy and Janet were waiting to make a pie. "I'd like to swim in the creek."

Mary Ellen cheerfully agreed, carrying both cans to the house, while I headed down the road, veering off through a stretch of nettles and ferns and then slipping two feet down the muddy bank to the water below. There, by the exposed roots of a large alder, I undressed and grabbed one of the inner tubes stashed by the stream. I stepped into the water gingerly, balancing on the smooth mossy rocks. A few yards from shore I slid onto the warm black rubber of the inner tube, leaned back, closed my eyes, and went with the flow, both the cosmic and the current. I drifted for a minute and then looked up at the trees arched above me. The sun shone through their leaves, dappling my body and the rippled water around me. I felt its heat on the bare skin of my breasts and belly and the nest of hair between my thighs. The cool water pulled at my legs and hands as they dangled over the edges of the inner tube. Everything smelled green and clean with a little undertow of musk from the dampness of the shore. I didn't need to think, just experience, expanding and enlarging, slowly merging into everything around me, light and airy, my psychic self released from solid form.

Adventure was everywhere and that was part of the thrill. Living together, things happened. Our house had one shower. We remodeled to a bath and a half by adding a sweat lodge near the tributary stream that flowed in front of it. First we cut branches and bent them to form a dome. Then we draped plastic over the frame to seal in the heat, "we" being the men. The women served more as a Greek chorus, supplying appreciative oohs and aahs to support the effort. Just being witness as well as naked was often enough to more than justify our presence. Next we covered the sweat lodge with blankets for added insulation and as a final touch an American flag was casually but deliberately draped over the top of the entire structure.

Like most events that summer, the wisp of an idea was the spark that caught fire. Decentralized and leaderless, we evoked action through query rather than command. Crazy Horse may have led the Lakota Sioux into battle with the cry *Hóka héy*, today is a good day to die, an affirmation of life by challenging fate. We, however, were sensualists, not warriors, seeking grandeur through pleasure, not pain. Our call to action, even as we identified with our Native American brethren, was for a milder form of rendezvous, presented in the languid drawl of a stoned and pacified hippie. When the stars aligned and our stench arose, the time was deemed propitious for a group cleanse. Guy took the lead. Seated on the cement steps of our front stoop, enjoying the peaceful effects of his most recent joint, he turned to Don next to him and uttered the words that challenged us to seize the moment.

"Hey Don, think today's a good day for a steam bath?"

"Sure enough," Don replied, cool as ever, and they set about gathering wood for a fire.

Clint meandered into view, followed by Hakim. All four scavenged for stones to load into the pit, and then sat back, smoked another joint, and contemplated the motion and color of the flames, heating rocks being the hippie version of watching a pot boil. Soon came the clarion call, "Steeeam Baaaath" shouted to the hills, several times in all directions, followed by the slow gathering of our clan and the rapid dispensing of our clothing. Mary Ellen and Janet ran into the house to get containers for water while Guy and Don moved the heated stones inside the sweat lodge. Wearing nothing but unlaced boots to protect their feet and mismatched work gloves to protect their hands, they poked and rolled each

*Steam bath, Greenleaf*

stone until it balanced in the middle of two rusty rebar poles. Grabbing the poles at opposite ends, they cautiously crossed the grassy stubble that lay between the fire and our polyester sauna. At the low opening to the hut, Guy and Don hunched over, bare butts out, scrotums dangling, and entered the cramped hot space. Negotiating step by step, they positioned their load, careful to avoid tripping as Guy maneuvered his way backwards around the glowing pit in the center. They communicated with each other through glances and grunts, lowering their arms in concert, keeping everything level. Inches above the pile Don nodded, the signal to slowly separate the rebar and deposit their load. Small chips flew off as the new rock landed, creating a shower of igneous sparks, one landing on Guy's boot. Guy teased Don as they backed out, cautioning him, "Don't trip, cuz 'Great Balls of Fire' is better as a song than an epithet." Then, still hunched and holding the awkward poles, they retreated, watchful of their steps and each other, until they were out, safe, and ready to set up again.

The pile inside grew until finally it was time for our *schvitz*. Like elephants in a parade we passed through the flap, crouching low, nose to naked butt, settling on stumps arranged around the curve of the lodge. I gasped with my first intake of the searing dry heat. Janet doused the rocks with water that diffused into clouds of mist, alternately hiding and revealing us to each other in the dim light.

"Hey, Yogadananda," Guy called out, ribbing Carol who, with a towel wrapped around her head, sat close to the bowl of water. Our ambiance was more convivial than spiritual. "Could you pour on some more?"

"Sure," Carol replied, spilling more than needed, inundating us with hot vaporized bursts.

"Whew, getting hot in here," Don said.

"Anyone remember to bring some sage to burn?" asked Janet. We bantered back and forth, checking each other out through the haze of steam and sweat, until after enough baths, we no longer saw when we looked. We were all family. We knew each other well. Finally the heat got too much to bear and Hak burst out, jumping into the adjacent stream. Everyone followed in spontaneous consensus, cleansed and united.

Life was bigger and more capacious than anything we had imagined. Plucking food from the earth made us children at the bosom of Mother Nature. By bathing together, we shed more than our clothes; we opened our pores to each other. In the creek we flowed with time and the current, drenched in our senses. Aloft in our tree houses we floated above the earth, no horizon line, just leaves and sky. Unbelievable, I thought. This is our life, every day, every week, Wednesday or Saturday, it's all the same.

Summer ended and winter approached. Fewer guests came through as work and school called them back to their regular lives. Carol headed back to New York with plans to return after a few months. For Hak and I, the change in weather meant an end to arboreal living. Tree houses had their limitations. After eight months of living communally, the idea of privacy began to hold some draw. Hakim and I staked out an old milk parlor, a concrete bunker built into the side of a low hill. Three of its walls abutted wet winter dirt. The remaining side had a small window that looked out over the surrounding pastures and woods. I placed two ivory netsuke on the rough sill, gifts from my parents, a memory of past lives. The milking parlor lacked insulation and heating. It had been a working space for cows, not an apartment. Short on cash and savvy, we installed a firebox from an old woodstove to keep us warm. It was inadequate for the job, and the job itself was impossible. Whatever heat we created was sucked into the porous cinderblocks and disappeared into the wet earth on their other side. I was sure that subterranean critters slinked and oozed in our direction, seeking comfort at the hearth we provided for them. For us, however, the damp cold inside did not feel that different from the grey chill outside. Lingering was a luxury. We needed to keep slowly turning next to the firebox, like hot dogs on a rotisserie, or tuck ourselves into bed with layers of covers pulled up around our necks. Hak and I shivered under a green cotton sleeping bag with red flannel lining that sported bowlegged cowboys and bucking broncos. In New Haven, when we bought it, the bag had seemed cozy. Now it was an artifact from another era, quaint but useless, a little like our marriage. From the outside it looked like it would keep us warm, but in truth we could not dispel the chill. Many more nights than not, we turned over, away from each other, and fell asleep, ending the day with the passionless goodwill of a pleasant "good-night." Maybe, I thought, we're just having a low spell. After all, every marriage has its ups and downs.

Highly motivated, I scrimped and saved and managed to pull together ninety-eight dollars, enough money to buy a good down bag from an Australian firm that had been touted in the *Whole Earth Catalogue*.

The bag was beautiful, a happy sea green that seemed full of Australian sunshine and frothy shoreline. I was very pleased with my purchase, the ideal confluence of the perfect tool at the right price, wrapped in the romance of far away places. My needs were simple. Satisfaction was pretty straightforward.

In winter, foggy clouds shrouded the hills, ever changing, never disappearing but shifting in depth and tone, hiding, then revealing, the distant outline of trees and peaks. The moisture had a life of its own, a study in gray, very gentle, always transforming, accompanied by a muted cacophony of frogs singing in the background. This was a safe and sensual world. I felt like a baby, cradled by the forested hills, swaddled in the gentle batting of the clouds and crooned to by an unseen chorale.

At no time did I ever consider going back to my old life, the one forged from respectability. The thought of being bound by rigid hours within a closed building dimmed my light and made me heavy. I had no regrets. In Greenleaf there were jobs to be done, responsibilities to the community, but I wanted to do them. Daily living was fun. Maybe it looked like we were doing nothing, but my life finally felt of value, to myself and to the larger world. I had been a student most of my life. For years, under buzzing fluorescent fixtures, I had parsed good literature, explored the sages, and sought answers through assigned readings. Now I lived inside the text. I was the story.

I was not the only person who felt this way. On a grey afternoon, soft and misty but still wet enough that it felt good to be inside, I found Clint, Guy, and Roggie seated at the empty table in the dining room, killing time, waxing philosophic. Guy took a deep toke of a joint and passed it to Clint while I warmed my hands around a chipped mug of home-blended yogi tea. Next to me Roggie cradled his forearm around a tin of government peanut butter, excavating its insides with a spoon. Clint sat back.

"When I was in the Navy I never imagined a life like this," he offered.

"I don't think any of us every imagined a life like this," snorted Roggie, taking a brief break from the peanut butter for some dope.

"But Clint's life was so different," Guy noted. "He's the only one of us who served, who actually signed up for the military."

"Strangely enough, it was in the Navy that I found out what it was like to be a member of the corporate world."

"What do you mean?" I asked, surprised. "Weren't you a pilot?" I had always thought about Clint in his other life with a little flutter, imagining him decked out in his flight suit with parachute straps wrapped between his legs, outlining his groin, his helmet under his arm. In my picture he was radiant in manly mystique, a technological warrior, steady and daring, risking his life and trusting his skills with every launch or landing of his jet on the high seas.

"I was an officer," he continued, "with a desk, a division, and responsibilities, people to oversee and make sure they performed relative to their job descriptions. Flying as a pilot was the recreational part."

"You mean it was mostly bureaucracy?" Guy sat up, incredulous. I, too, was having a hard time imagining Clint in a tailored, tightly buttoned uniform behind a desk filling out paperwork.

Clint nodded. "All that changed when I got out of the Navy and went back to college. I thought life there was pretty good, improving myself, not being stuck in a routine."

"It's funny," Roggie interjected. "I left college to get out of a routine."

Guy laughed and nodded his head knowingly, handing the tail end of the joint to Clint, who held it pinched between his thumb and index finger, momentarily lost in thought.

"While I was there I read the Tolkien trilogy and started to think about alternate lifestyles. For me that was a big part of coming here to Oregon." He stopped for a moment. I had never heard Clint talk about this before.

"After all, what did the system have to offer us, some chump change and a few token bits of freedom tossed in our direction for a couple of weeks each year?"

"I get your point," agreed Roggie a little reluctantly, "but then again, what's freedom?" Roggie saw himself as en route to somewhere else. Oregon was not his final destination.

"Being part of a community does feel good and living on the farm is fun when we aren't miserable, cold, or hungry, but something seems off."

"I love living here," I interjected, sitting up tall on the bench, my dirty fingernails splayed out on the rough boards of the table.

"That's not the point, Margaret. Here we are, highly intelligent, very driven people, checking out. We do all the hippie things first class, as is our nature, except this life is not our natural habitat."

"Maybe for you, but this is starting to look like my natural habitat more and more each day," Guy drawled.

"Look at us," Roggie continued, "educated achievers with well-developed skills that need flexing but are superfluous in this back-to-the-earth movement."

"We are changing, Roggie. We are learning," I said, my frizzy hair jouncing as I turned to look first at Guy and then at Clint for support.

"True, but maybe the skills and intelligence needed in the country are not my strong suit. Clint has them in spades, but not everyone else. Where does that leave the rest of us?"

It was a good question that went up in smoke.

Outside the farm, in the world we thought we left behind, the country continued to unravel. Congress extended the draft for another two years. Vietnam veterans threw away their medals. The Weather Underground exploded a bomb in the Capitol. Lieutenant Calley stood trial for the My Lai Massacre. All of it felt distant to me. We didn't get a newspaper, had no television, and our interest in the rest of the world was minimal. Hakim was not in danger of being drafted. Clint had already served, Guy took care of it earlier, and Don was 4-F for health reasons. That left Roggie, whose letter found him at Greenleaf.

"Guess what I got today?" Roggie teased me, clearly wanting to talk. We were hanging over the fence watching our dog Bitcho run circles around the cattle in our pasture, hoping they might join him in a game of chase. Just his antics were amusing enough for us on this slow afternoon.

"I don't know. A check from *The Millionaire*?"

"Come on, Margaret."

"Okay. You're dying to tell me. What did you get today?"

"My draft notice. I've been called up and need to report for a physical."

That took all the play out of the afternoon.

"What are you going to do?" I asked, concerned for his safety.

"I'm going to try the albumin in the urine trick."

"Is it a sure thing?"

"It better be. My only back-up is allergies."

"You're allergic?"

"When I was ten I had a severe reaction to some fish."

It seemed like a pretty flimsy barrier between life and the draft to me.

A few days later Roggie returned from Portland. I ran to meet him on our road.

"Did it work?"

"Not as I planned." he replied cryptically.

"Not as you planned?" My voice started to rise.

"Just listen, Margaret."

This was not always easy for me, but I realized he had a story to tell. I shut my mouth and did my job, witness to his adventure.

"I stayed up half the night before my review, trying to dissolve the albumin. No one told me it wasn't soluble. I managed to mix up a little which I poured into a vial and snuck in with me. Once I was naked, I realized I didn't have a chance. There was nothing to do but play it straight."

"Without anything?"

Roggie continued, precise and even in his delivery. "I told the doctor about my allergy history. He asked about swelling. When I told him yes, he said I was at risk for anaphylactic shock. With that he signed me off. Get this. It's a legitimate deferment; 1-Y, not 4-F."

"No."

"I couldn't believe it either. My first instinct was to shake the guy's hand and thank him, to jump up and down and yell, 'I'm free. I'm going to live.' Then I realized I'd better get out of there as fast as I could before somebody changed their mind."

Evidently we were not as far out as we thought.

# PART III

## Floras Creek

*The main cabin at Floras Creek at the time of purchase*

# CHAPTER 13 Rocky Mountain High

OUR ONE-YEAR LEASE FOR THE FARM was running out and we needed a new home, preferably a permanent one. Carol wanted to purchase property. She had returned again with this in mind. The solution to both quests merged on a coastal mountain where Carol found 160 pristine acres populated by bears, cougars, and the government hunters that stalked them, thinning the wildlife so that domesticated animals could thrive. We were equally wary of all three. Shorty, the previous owner, had cleared a football-sized field on a gently rounded hill. There he built his one-room cabin, ringed by the forest, anchoring the top of the property. Floras Creek ran through the lower forty acres, a half-hour hike down the mountain through towering trees and tiny meadows. Water, along with timber, was valuable. The creek was the gold that demarked the lower boundaries of the property, running cold and clear, over rocks and under roots, forming waterfalls and collecting pools, some deep enough for swimming. All of this was now Carol's. She had dreamed of green pastures and a cozy house, one where she could plug in a toaster or catch a few sitcoms. Instead, with Clint's urging, she bought her own national park, perfect for his mountain-man capabilities.

We moved with enthusiasm, ignoring potentials difficulties. There were no group discussions about membership or ownership. Each of us painted our private visions, embellishing them with what we wanted to see. Not too different from falling in love. I imagined that we would continue as before, but at a new location generously purchased for us by Carol. Hak and I never discussed any other possibility. The move grabbed our attention and drove us all forward. We had one month to prepare.

Although the drive south from Greenleaf to Floras Creek took only two hours on the coastal highway, we entered new terrain. At the town of Langlois, not much more than a bar and a few houses, we turned east and headed inland, driving up the mountain on a winding logging road that was paved for the first five miles. We ascended in vehicles that ran on hope and Clint's mechanical expertise, always keeping alert, especially when the asphalt ended. The foothills were open pasture, home to herds of local sheep. At the sound of our trucks they would panic and run onto the road in front of us, a roiling mass of wooly haunches on tiny cloven hooves. Our view was of puffy butts dangling dingleberries and twigs, quivering as the sheep high-tailed it as fast as their ungainly pace could take them, braying mournfully all the way. They never turned off the pavement. Instead the sheep stampeded straight ahead until some signal in the landscape spoke to the lead animals. At this mysterious clue, the whole flock turned as one, off the road and across the hills, fleeing to safer pastures. At first the stampede was exciting, but over time these encounters became the equivalent of being stuck in rush hour traffic; there you were until they weren't, frustrating unless you had no agenda and could get into the zen of the experience.

Past the sheep, we shifted gears and climbed into the forested hills of the mountain, where loggers still actively stripped the cash crop. As we rounded each bend in the narrow road, we never knew if we would confront a forty-ton logging truck, tall as a house and headed straight for us. A fully loaded Peterbilt bearing down on us, its hulking pyramid of logs looming ten feet over the cab, was a heart-stopping experience. Vigilance was necessary.

Ten miles up the road we arrived at the base of the rutted path that led up to our central clearing. From there we continued on foot. In a strong truck with powerful gears, it was possible to slowly crawl and bump our way up, but the ride was laborious and kidney wrenching, a challenge for both the vehicle and its driver. Out of necessity we walked, about a ten-minute hike in good weather, not that any of us still had a watch, as time had lost all meaning. The path cut through hillsides banked with low brush, prehistoric ferns, and slender saplings. In spring, wildflowers burst with color. Digitalis sported speckled purple and white trumpet flowers. Tiny bleeding hearts, pink and delicate, peeked from under the leaves of white fairy bells. Yellow wood violets brightened the undergrowth wherever sunshine filtered through. There was no need to pick blossoms and arrange them in a vase to decorate our lives. The scale of things had turned upside down. We moved inside a living, well-tended floral arrangement, small beings in the vastness of nature's terrarium.

Before our move, Clint, Guy, Don, and Hakim made several trips to clean up debris and get us established. During the years that the cabin was vacant, critters had moved in and humans had acted out. The guys described to the rest of us how all the windows were smashed and the doors at either end of the cabin hung loosely on their hinges. Junk and trash lay a foot deep on the floor. Shorty, the previous owner, collected paperback westerns to pass away his long lonely nights. There were three or four hundred of them scattered about, moldering from rain, vandalism, and woodland creatures. Our advance party slept outside the first two nights.

Once things were clean, it was time to move in. Two trucks took off from Greenleaf loaded with tools, supplies, and a chipped, cast-iron woodstove. Now we were really country, no more electric cooking. Preparations took place in early February and that meant weather, one of those Oregon coastal storms where the winds blow about fifty miles an hour and the rain comes down sideways. Getting up the mountain road was a challenge, especially with faulty windshield wipers, tires way past their prime, and spark plugs more ready to miss than hit. Poverty, even self-imposed, creates challenges. In the blind blackness of that storm, I knew every set of eyes scanned for the road's edge. No one wanted to go over.

At home we waited anxiously. There were no phones to assure us of the safety of our men or to inform us of their impending arrival. Did everything go easily or had some problems arisen? I sat at the dinning room table at Greenleaf with Mary Ellen, Janet, and Carol. The afternoon light was grey. Each of us nursed a cup of tea made from foraged mint as we speculated on the return of our men. Grinding gears interrupted our talk. We heard doors slam and the sound of familiar voices. "They're back," Mary Ellen called, running to the door. There they were, our guys, dirty and bedraggled, pleased with themselves and happy to be home. We greeted them like explorers back from the unknown.

"Sit down and rest."

"I'll get you some warm tea."

"You're covered in dirt. What a mess."

"What was the place like?"

We gathered round, full of happiness at their safe arrival, ready to be titillated by the telling of the tale.

The four men sat down at the table, oblivious to the crusted, dried mud that flaked off their boots and Levis. They started to talk, hirsute griots, weaving the story that would become part of our family history.

Clint opened slowly, drawing us into their circle.

"Driving up the mountain was all we could manage. The trucks wouldn't make it over that last hill. We had to leave them fully loaded at the side of the logging road."

"Water was just pouring down the path. We had no traction. Our wheels kept spinning, throwing out rocks and mud," Don added, picking up the beat.

"Walking was the only choice left," Guy said, his eyes bright with the adventure. "We needed to get to the cabin, but we had the stove."

"I don't know why we didn't just wait for morning," interjected Don dryly.

"We were afraid of losing the stove and wanted to get the job done," added Hakim, loving the memory of the adventure.

Don continued. "So there we were, stuck, standing around in the dark with just a few flashlights, rain blowing everywhere, wet and cold in spite of our slickers and boots. We got the motherfucker off the truck. That was the easy part."

"Yeah," Hakim interjected. "Then we had to lug that fucker up two steep hills. We carried it like you would a tiger after a hunt, tied onto a pole. Two guys were on each end staggering under the weight of all that iron."

"It was Clint's idea," Guy clarified.

"Fine for him," said Hakim. "He was in front with Don. I was with Guy in the back. The whole miserable way up, I was hoping that it was lashed on tight and wouldn't slide back on us."

"I don't know how we did it, staggering and grunting through the mud like that," Guy added. "The rocks were so slippery. It was hard to get a foot hold, let alone see where we were going." He grinned and shook his head. "We weren't heading back down again that night."

The tale didn't deter me. Just the opposite, it whetted my appetite. We owned this land. Our guys were courageously working together to prepare it for the rest of us. I was thrilled about having a permanent home in the woods where the men went first and the women and children followed.

Our final exodus south was a cross between the dustbowl diaspora of the Depression and peasants on the move. We draped our flatbed truck, which had jerry- rigged plywood sides, with a tarp. I rode in the back, along with Rocky and Janet, as well as our dining table, three benches, loose tools, jumbled household items, trash bags full of clothes, a few crates filled with chickens, and two tethered goats. We humans dangled our legs over the back end and watched the scenery recede, trying not to breathe the exhaust that wafted up from the tailpipe. Nestled with friends and livestock, inhaling noxious gases, I was ready for the next phase of our utopian experiment.

*The interior of the main cabin at Floras Creek during the first months*

Like any new owners, we needed to upgrade and remodel a bit. Clint and Don laid boards across the rafters, under the peaked roof of the cabin, forming a makeshift sleeping loft, a bedroom for us all. Talk about communal. We knew the arrangement was temporary, but it might take a few months before the weather cleared and we could build more private alternatives. Clint installed an iron hand pump on the rough plank countertop that surrounded our wooden sink, providing inside plumbing. The curved black handle and spout were elegant in line and mechanical simplicity. With the flex of a bicep we could pull water from our well, no bucket or exposure to the elements needed.

We slept, cooked, cleaned, plotted, planned, sponge-bathed, and ate, all in that tiny cabin. Every task took time, complicated by the number of people sharing the space and the level of technology. At Greenleaf we simply turned on the hot water and added a little soap to clean up from dinner. Here we cut down a tree, the first step, it seemed, in almost any task. Then we chopped wood, lit a fire, pumped water, and heated it. That was the prep for washing dirty dishes. Once the fire was up and burning we had to continually tend it while we boiled more water for rinsing our cracked plates and home-turned bowls. We dipped our dishes clean in a fresh basin and then let them drain, balanced one on top of the other on the counter. Finished, we emptied our dirty water into the wooden sink. The drain was a hose that ran through one of the floorboards and then snaked down a small incline, emptying away from the cabin. No wonder we no longer wore watches. Like legendary kings who squandered gold and jewels, we had a surfeit of time and spent it freely, luxuriating in the indulgence. Everything slowed down. The technology demanded it. Kerosene lanterns were our only light, not just conceits in the face of electricity as they could be at Greenleaf. In February, darkness fell at 5:00 and it landed with a thud, forcing us inside, restricted to small pools of glowing light that pulled us toward each other. To get along in such tight quarters you needed to be mellow. Dope was a necessity. Last summer's harvest from Greenleaf carried us through. I, of course, did it straight, not too hard a task, as by this time I was a true convert, dedicated to the cause.

We shared the cabin for several months until the weather dried and we could stake out individual sites. Hakim and I chose a clearing up from the main cabin, open to the sky, surrounded by ferns and enclosed by larger brush and alder. There we built a platform for our pup tent. What a tiny, tidy little dwelling, our own place, with just enough room for our sleeping bags to open into a double bed, and a wood box supporting a lantern at our heads. Floras Creek was a new beginning, hopefully for Hakim and me as well. We snuggled in our tent, zipped in and cozy, sweet with each other in our newfound privacy. There was no place else I wanted to be.

# CHAPTER 14  Leaving on a Jet Plane

WITH NO AMENITIES, EVERY DAILY TASK WAS A CHALLENGE. Not everyone was as satisfied as Hak and I. Brandi and Fairchild became collateral damage within the first month, opting to move to Eugene where having a baby, but no man, was not such a formidable challenge, Lev by this time having decamped. Pampers were expensive and washing soiled cloth diapers was much like doing the dishes, chopping wood and heating water the first steps. Tasks became divided to some degree along gender lines and anatomy became destiny.

By April we lost a few more. Guy and Janet left for warmer climes and a more spiritual quest, heading south to the Self-Realization Fellowship started by Paramahansa Yoganada. Roggie decided to follow his dream, heading east to Indonesia on liberated plane tickets, his boat a casualty of excessive optimism and the move to Floras Creek.

Through the hippie underground we had acquired international airline tickets for ninety dollars, domestic ones for less—real tickets, stolen from travel agencies, completely blank. As a full-service entrepreneur, our connection also sold us a book that listed all airline flights and their codes, a necessary resource for the completion of our illegal dealings. We chose to see the tickets as liberated, not stolen, a critical difference. Greedy corporations and big government were the thieves. Stealing from the rich and giving to the poor was a moral act.

Don, Mary Ellen, Roggie, and I bought tickets and then pooled our cash for the booking guide. Roggie was the first to give the scam a try. We sat around our table and studied the flight book, figuring out codes and routes. He made his choices and then came my part. Tickets were still hand-filled at that time and it was necessary to mark each blank box on the complex coupon with the precise numbers and cryptic anagrams of Roggie's flight. The catch was that someone other than Roggie had to do the writing. Feeling a bit nervous as an accessory to a crime and briefly conjuring big police and little me, I carefully copied letters and numbers into all the right boxes, double-checking for any amateurish mistake that might give the whole thing away. Finished, I looked up and asked Roggie, "Aren't you scared?"

Always level, he replied true to form.

"No, not scared, resigned. What's going to happen will happen. I do need to get some kind of travel outfit, though. Doing this looking like a hippie would be madness."

A week or so later, Roggie came back from town with his costume.

"Look at this. It only cost a dollar," he said, unfolding a long cloth purchased at the Goodwill store. "I can drape it as a turban to hide my long hair." He was excited by his own ingenuity. "I also bought a black sports coat to make me look more respectable." Using the scratched mirror tacked to the wall of the cabin, Roggie wound the light fabric around his head, preening and tucking until it was just right, his beard the only hair left to see. Happy with the results, he reached for his new jacket, completing his transformation, a western Sikh, modest and unassuming, before the days of international terrorism. "What do you think?" he asked. "For someone who doesn't want to attract too much attention, is this outfit just a giant neon sign meep-meeping 'weirdo, weirdo'?"

"Could be," I said. "But you don't really have much choice, do you. Just don't turn me in if you get caught."

When we bought the tickets, we were instructed to alter our booking at the first stop in our trip. In the innocent world before computers, we could reduce our risk simply by changing our itinerary. One rescheduling and we were in possession of a new, professionally issued ticket, making it harder to track the original fraud.

Roggie left for the first leg of his journey, Copenhagen, and after a few days of sightseeing headed toward Japan, stopping in Athens en route. He wanted to make the most of his travel opportunity as well as cover his trail, careful to leave no scent for the airlines. From Athens, Roggie flew to Tokyo, his route taking him right over Vietnam. This was 1972, the height of the war. Roggie wrote us that he looked out his window, pressed his head against the pane, and studied the tropical forest below. A clearing appeared in the green coastal plain and Danang, one of Vietnam's largest cities, came into view, a major center of operations for the American military, providing a base for aerial attacks against the enemy. Just a few years earlier, North Vietnamese troops had inundated the city in their surprise Tet offensive, a brutal battle costly in lives on both sides. Roggie realized that could have been his future. Here was Danang, viewed from the safety of a passing commercial airline instead of up-close and under fire. Roggie looked down, one allergy attack away from what might have been.

One traveler was gone. Don and Mary Ellen wanted to follow. Their plan was to build a geodesic dome, popularized by the environmental visionary Buckminster Fuller, to house their belongings while they leisurely explored the world on their purloined tickets. Upon their return, they would have a place to live with everything they needed safely stored and waiting. Instead of a temporary structure, they envisioned making their dome from concrete.

The permanent nature of this structure, even if it was Buckminster Fuller–inspired, became the fulcrum on which their fate was determined. Clint and Carol were now landowners. A quiet shift had been put into place with the signing of the deed, the ripples of which took a while to reach the shore.

Don and Mary Ellen's plan was the first stone cast into the surface of that pond. All of a sudden who could build what, and where, had become an issue. I was firing up the wood stove, heating some water, when Rocky came rushing into the main cabin with the news.

"Did you hear? Clint had a fight with Don and Mary Ellen. He told them they had to leave."

Could this be true? Were we coming apart? Was Mary Ellen that annoying? Sure she had a sing-song voice, walked on her tiptoes, and seemed slavishly devoted to Don, but she could also be very sweet. We weren't close, but that didn't matter. They were part of us. I was upset and strode off to find Clint. He was hand-sawing some small branches not too far from the site Don and Mary Ellen had selected.

"Hey, Clint," I called. He stopped and turned to face me.

"Why did you tell Don and Mary Ellen to leave?" I demanded.

"I didn't tell Don to leave at all," he explained with a slightly defensive air.

"Everyone is talking down at the main cabin. They said you told them they had to go."

"Look Margaret, they wanted to build some big concrete thing and leave."

"But it was a Buckminster Fuller dome."

"It doesn't matter. It was going to be big and heavy, more a blight than part of the land."

"So, you did tell them to leave," I said, wanting clarification.

"No, I had a heart-to-heart with Don, let him know that he couldn't build something that permanent here." Clint's voice was measured, deliberate but firm. He had a way of telling things so that they balanced right on top of the fence, not quite falling one way or the other, unless he got mad. If Clint was really pushed, he could lash out with a brutal temper—cold, sharp, a laser beamed right at you. He didn't get to that point often, but you knew he could.

"Carol and I own the land. I didn't want to have to demolish a concrete dome at some future date. Don was nice about it."

My stance softened as I imagined a massive mushroom cap of concrete filling the space where we stood. I understood what Clint was saying. I also got what he wasn't saying. Things had shifted. We had hit our first pothole, ownership. Don and Mary Ellen were just the harbingers of things to come, but like most signs, it was hard to decipher, except in retrospect. This was all confusing to me, and I sought out Guy and Janet back at the main cabin. Don and Mary Ellen were there, rolling up their sleeping bags and stuffing clothes into an old army surplus bag. I wanted to tell them not to go, to say I was sorry, to ask what happened. They looked pretty shaken.

"I wish you would stay," I offered.

Don stopped tightening the strap around his bag and turned toward me. "My dad warned me."

"About what?" I loved his dad and mom. They were so kind to us all.

"About what just happened," he replied bitterly. "When I told my dad about the new land and how we were all going to live on it, building homes and a future together, he was skeptical. 'Why would you put money into a home on some property you don't own?' he asked me." Don stood straight, straddling his bag, and looked past me for a moment, listening to an interior dialogue. Then he quickly bent over to resume packing. "Stupidly I wrote him off," he muttered angrily.

"Yeah, you told him he just didn't understand," Mary Ellen added.

"What a fool I was. I told him we were a family, that all of us were in this together." Mary Ellen put her hand on Don's back but he shook it off.

"Today I had to eat my own words," he said, his mouth curling with rancor and self disgust.

"We don't need this place," Mary Ellen jumped in quickly. She was fiercely loyal to Don. "There're other things we want to do."

"You know what's the hardest?" he asked, more to himself then either of us.

"What?" I asked.

"My dad was right."

Don and Mary Ellen disappeared. They packed up and left as fast as they could, the surface of our life sealing quickly over the rift. I didn't know what to do, so did nothing. Hakim was upset about it but not ready to do much more than grumble. After all, nobody forced Don and Mary Ellen to leave. We ignored this bump in the road, an anomaly; it could never happen to us.

Clint was torn. Don was his friend. The land may have belonged to Carol, but he was her consort. Now he was caught between his vested interests and the subterranean rumblings in the group. Clint needed support, someone with whom he could talk. When Carol was traveling back and forth between New York and Oregon, tension had risen between them. I was frequently Clint's confidant as he tried to make sense of his relationship. Here we were again, me listening as Clint sorted things out.

"One of the things I liked about Greenleaf was that no one was making any rules. That appealed to me. In the military there was nothing but regulations, and you obeyed them or you ended up in jail."

"Hak tries to organize things, but we are all too egocentric to follow," I said laughing, trying to lighten the mood. But Clint needed to dig deeper.

"At the farm there was such enthusiasm and heart it never occurred to me there might be a time when somebody would have to move on. The word *no* was never used." He shifted on the stump outside the main cabin and was silent for a moment.

"This thing with Don and Mary Ellen is a turning point, but I don't know what else I could have done."

We both sat there, contemplating the wood chips at our feet, while the tap-tap-tapping of a woodpecker, busy building his nest, echoed from the forest.

## CHAPTER 15 Family Affair

THOSE WE LOST THROUGH ATTRITION were replaced by new arrivals. All you had to do was show up. No Bedouin in the Empty Quarter could have been more hospitable to brethren traveling the desert sands of the straight world. Class lines disappeared—at least we tried to erase them. Guests ranged from the mentally infirm to the lonely and lost, including family and friends. A few gems were tucked in there as well. Georgia, en route from Texas to medical school at McGill University, stopped by to visit and stayed through the summer. She was bright, hard-working, and very good company.

Clint's brother Stuart arrived in April in his 1954 Ford pickup, complete with dented camper shell and two dogs. He had left New Haven with the rest of us but wintered in Colorado, earning money as a pick-up carpenter. Stuart arrived with a frozen turkey in hand, an offering and an apology, as he had planned to join us for Thanksgiving in Greenleaf. There was an odd logic and sweetness in that turkey, but that was Stuart. Clint said that something in Stu changed after he got out of Vietnam. Whatever it was, it made no dent in his appeal to women—they loved him.

I was in front of my tent platform shaking out the sleeping bag that served as our quilt when Carol stopped by, laughing, an empty wooden bowl under her arm.

"Hey Margaret, guess what?" she asked, continuing without waiting for a reply. "I took some cookies up to Stuart. He's cutting wood in the hills over there, and you'll never believe this." Carol collapsed next to my tent and gasped for breath, she was laughing so hard. "When I got there . . . when I found him . . . she . . . Mary Ellen . . ." Carol could hardly speak. "She was there . . . Mary Ellen was already there . . . and she was holding a plate of cookies too." Carol lost it again. "She had her own cookies. We were busted. I looked down at my cookies in my bowl and I laughed so hard. All I could think of was, 'next thing you know there'll be a line.'"

"What did Stuart do?"

"Nothing, of course, he's a Helvey, that's their charm, cowboys. Stuart just stood there, a little embarrassed, while Mary Ellen and I looked at each other, surprised at being exposed. It was so funny."

"Carol, he's Clint's brother!"

*Stuart and Molly*

"Oh come on, Margaret, I'm not going to do anything. But he sure is good looking."

Our next new arrivals were the Greeks: Paul, Katrina, and their three-year-old son, Kokia. Paul, another architect, was friends with Clint from Texas and New Haven. He was slight, with long black hair, a dark beard, and deep-set eyes that drew you into his very internal world. Katrina, in contrast, had straight red hair that hung past her waist, not as big a task as it might seem as she was barely more than five feet tall. She had an open face with a few freckles and warm, gold-brown eyes. Just twenty-one years old, ten years younger than Paul, Katrina looked like a child herself, but there was no mistaking her competence, a balance to the dreamer in her husband. And then there was Kokia, a little man, a precise prince, compact, dark and intense like his father, just a younger version, combining the energy of a four-year-old and the vocabulary of an adult. They were our first real intact family with a child who talked and walked, one who really counted, not a babe in arms. This was quite an addition. Clint had invited them to stop by and they stayed for several years. Paul was extending his stay in the United States to avoid returning to Greece, which was now in the hands of the right wing junta. I did not know them in New Haven but was thrilled to have another woman join our group, particularly one as capable, warm, and perceptive as Katrina.

"What brought you here?" I asked Katrina as we straightened up the main cabin one afternoon, truly curious, as she did not have hippie written on her anywhere.

"Paul and I had some troubles and thought a new beginning in Hawaii would be a good idea. We hitchhiked to California and took a detour here to visit Clint." Katrina relayed this information in her matter-of-fact style, grimacing slightly at a dirty dish she had found under the table.

"You hitchhiked with a child? Weren't you worried that something might happen?"

"Not really."

I could hardly believe what I was hearing.

"We did have some adventures though. One night we camped on the beach and there was this crazy person just back from Vietnam." Katrina sat down and took Kokia, who was never far from her side, on her lap. "Paul stayed up the whole night talking with him, trying to keep awake, making sure we weren't attacked while we were sleeping."

"And you didn't tell Paul that you were done, over, this trip had come to an end? After all, you had a child with you."

"No. I wasn't scared, not even later when three men who had just been released from jail gave us a ride. I don't know if they were out legally or not, but they were very nice to us, especially protective of me for some reason and very playful with Kokia."

I watched her nuzzle her son, such a good mother, but clearly Katrina was full of surprises.

"While we were camping we ran into another group that looked like Eagle Scouts on an outing. They were from juvenile hall. Some social workers were taking them out for a weekend."

"Didn't you meet anyone who wasn't crazy or a criminal?" I asked.

She seemed philosophical about the situation. "Remember the guys who drove us here and stayed for a few days?"

"Sure, they seemed nice enough."

"Those were the ones just out of jail."

"You brought them here?"

"Actually, they were quite shocked. They couldn't believe there were so many college graduates here."

"Those guys were surprised about us?"

"Yes, they didn't expect everyone to be so educated."

I had to think about this for a moment. "Evidently we've all got our own prejudices," I said and shrugged.

"The only person who made me nervous was the guy on the beach," Katrina continued, "the Vietnam vet, but Paul took care of that."

Katrina may have been small, but she was unflappable, a trait that served her well in her relationship with her husband.

For Paul, being in Floras Creek was a childhood fantasy come true, a chance to live out the myth of the American West, something he dreamed about as a boy growing up in Athens. Here was wild country, vast spaces peopled with legends different from those of the rocky isles of the Aegean. The pace of life was familiar, though: no external demands, just those you created for yourself, a magical place where you could live with very little pressure, particularly if your wife was a practical and devoted mother.

Paul and Katrina arrived our first summer in Floras Creek and set up residence in an old army tent pitched in the forest. The tent was small, set on a platform of wood rounds covered with scavenged siding, too short

*Katrina, pregnant, at Floras Creek*

to accommodate even Paul's modest height. By early fall the rainy season began and water rushed beneath their feet, frustrating Katrina but leaving Paul unconcerned. He loved living in the woods and could not fathom Katrina's annoyance. To keep the tent warm, Paul installed a small wood stove, cutting a hole for the pipe, which ultimately became a vent for almost all of the heat they worked so hard to generate. Katrina hit her limit and the family temporarily moved into the loft of the main cabin until Paul built a place for them. As inertia was Paul's default mode, this took a year to happen. In the duration, long conversations in Greek floated down, letting any one sitting in the cabin below know through tone, if not content, that all was not well in paradise.

Our international tentacles reached deep. During our second summer, Paul's brother George arrived from Greece for a visit, followed a few years later by Hamdan, Hak's youngest sibling, who arrived from Indonesia and stayed. I didn't know George was expected. He appeared as I gardened alone, sitting in the dirt, topless, soaking up the welcomed warmth of June. Glancing up, I saw someone emerge from the path that led from the road, a silhouette that, unlike those of my loved ones, was unfamiliar. Gradually it became clear the figure was a man, cleaner and neater than any of our usual guests. He continued to advance. I watched from my spot on the ground, making note of his khaki pants and plaid shirt, apprehension building. There were just the two of us in the heat of the high noon sun. He moved closer, coming within fifty yards of the garden. What to do? Should I rush to where I had discarded my shirt and pull it on? Definitely not cool, we were way beyond that. Or should I sit here naked from the waist up, my breasts blowing in the breeze, and greet this stranger? I was starting to feel this was a disturbing dream, the classic prototype where the dreamer is nude in a crowd of people, all of whom are clothed. My discomfort rose. Equally uncomfortable, however, was admitting to myself that being half nude with a fully clothed stranger felt creepy. Now it was a face-off. Not between the stranger and me, but within myself. Which part of me would prevail? I made my decision. Rising from the ground, I reached out to shake hands with Paul's brother George, clean-cut, neatly dressed, fresh from Greece, and thinking he had landed in hog heaven, or at least a performance of real living theatre.

In addition to welcoming new members, we made new friends. Up the coast was another group centered around two brothers, Gino and Lester, a distinctive pair, with long dark hair and full black beards. Together they looked like the Smith Brothers of cough drop fame—that is, if the Smith Brothers had been bikers, less effete, more working class, and definitely into drugs of another order. They lived with their clan in a gutted ranch house, way past disrepair, with a ping-pong table holding pride of place in the main room and not much else to keep it company except for a few mismatched, well-sprung chairs. The kitchen looked as if it had been stripped for a remodel that never took place, lacking in everything including appliances. A double burner hot plate with food-encrusted coils straddled two chairs and served as the stove.

Gino had been a hair dresser in the Bay Area, but it was easy to imagine him, minus the beard, in a black and white Fellini film walking over dusty Sicilian hills with a goat, a rough loaf of bread and a chunk of cheese under his arm. Like any good hairdresser, Gino was easy with people. In contrast, his beautiful, delicate wife Sue, a dancer, was distant, lost in the aura of her own heavy drug reality, out of place and out of mind in the chaos of their lives. Reba, their angelic three-year-old daughter, had an undulating scar over most of her left shoulder and upper chest, the result of coming too close to a pot of boiling water on the jerry-rigged hot plate. Being a child was hard where there were no grown-ups.

Lester was another story; there was no dropping far enough out to lose the biker vibe beneath his hippie exterior. He was bigger in height and girth than Gino and even more bedecked with hair. On self-proclaimed festive occasions, Lester tied little ribbons in his full black beard, tiny colorful bows setting off, rather than softening, the slightly dangerous edge he exuded.

These neighbors, our brothers and sisters, were graduates of the street, an elite institution in its own right. They too loved the land, the ideal of community, and the thrill of adventure, but they were as different from us as the crowd at Stormy's, our local bar in Langlois. What brought us together were drugs, our shared outlaw status, and the dream of more than what the ordinary offered. They heard the same silent call that mesmerized us to the point of giving up everything we knew. Like us their efforts were bumbling, but in different ways.

We visited them from time to time, but I never felt quite comfortable at their place, the darkness of heavy drugs felt if not seen. I worked hard to overcome my reservations, embarrassed that they might be based on class and not consciousness. Over time I grew to enjoy the warmth and vitality of Gino, the most open member of their troupe. The contrast between his almost childlike openness and the dreary shadows of their communal life confused and fascinated me.

# CHAPTER 16  Get It While You Can

OUR NEW ROUTINES BEGAN TO FALL INTO PLACE. With the start of summer the weather was warm and dry, winter and wetness still months away. Hak and I, snug in our tent at night, spent most of our daylight hours busy with everyone except each other. Added to our slow movement away from each other and into the community was the fact that out of necessity the group's activities tended to break down along gender lines, something we modern women chose not to look at too closely, grateful that there were men to saw, chop, build, and take care of all the heavy lifting we couldn't do. Men and women alike were appreciative of what the other had to offer and there was more than enough excitement to go around. Each day dawned differently. Change was always percolating.

Carol and I planned a trip into Eugene for supplies as well as an overnight stay at Footbridge. We at Floras Creek, in turn, hosted some of their people for a few days, including Kathy, a single woman relatively new to their group. Intra-communal visiting was somewhere between English country squires spending extended stays at each other's estates and third-world inhabitants traveling to the clan home on donkey back, complete with live chickens. To call on another group meant staying more than one night and bringing something to add to the larder.

Our errands done and visit over, Carol and I tooled along the highway heading home. I was at the wheel. Traveling was safer that way. Carol's spatial sense, particularly in a moving vehicle, made me nervous. We drove silently for a few miles, each of us very comfortable in the presence of the other. Something had been on my mind, and in the meditative quiet of the drive it started to bother me again.

"I bet he slept with her while we were gone," I said.

"Who?" Carol said.

"Hakim."

"Slept with who?"

"Kathy, that woman visiting from Footbridge."

"Her? What makes you think that?" Carol warmed up to the timeless topic at hand.

"I just have a feeling. They were hanging around together before we left."

"I didn't see anything."

"Yeah well, if it's not Clint, what do you know?"

"True."

"Something was there."

"Is that okay with you?" Carol asked. She was attuned to the openness of the times, but in her gut she felt the threat another woman imposed no matter what the rhetoric.

"I don't like it," I said. "But there's not much I can do about it. So he sleeps with her once. It's not the end of the world." I was trying to hedge my bets and cover all possibilities, anything but face the betrayal it might mean.

Back home, Carol and I dropped off our groceries at the main cabin, proud of what we had gleaned from the day-old shelves and discarded produce behind the store. We visited with Clint and Stu, who were sharpening tools. I asked after Hak but they said they hadn't seen him around. A little edgy, I walked up the hill and through the trees to our tent. Hakim was not there. I unpacked and cleaned out the leaves and fir needles that continually invaded our tent. Hearing footsteps on the path, I turned. Hakim came toward me in his jeans and heavy boots, his hair tied back in a ponytail and a look on his face that told me nothing.

"Hi. What's been going on?" I asked. He didn't look guilty, apologetic, worried, or in any way uncomfortable. I relaxed.

"It feels good to be home," I offered.

"Margaret," Hak said, and then paused for a brief beat. Something shifted in that space. My body became alert, aware that incoming ordnance was about to explode.

"I'm leaving."

"You're what?" This wasn't even on my radar.

"I'm moving in with Kathy at Footbridge."

"You're moving in with Kathy?" I repeated dumbfounded. There was no place to put this piece of information. That was it? No explanation. Nothing. Just, "I'm leaving."

"That's what I need to do. I came back to get my things and pack up. She's waiting down on the logging road for me."

I watched as Hak packed up his few belongings. He took his clothes, stuffing them into a small backpack, and rolled up the plaid wool blanket my parents had brought back from a trip to Scotland. I just stood there, my mind blank. Hakim turned away and somberly headed down the path to Kathy. I sat down on our tent platform in front of the triangle of mosquito netting that was the doorway to our home and stared at the clearing where Hakim had just disappeared. Then my shock wore off and rage set in. Where is that motherfucker? He needs to deal with *me*. I ran down the path, my boots pounding on the dirt through the tunnel of trees. Everything opened and I could see the clearing with the main cabin and the surrounding woods in the distance. About five feet below, Hakim, head down, continued his trek toward Kathy and away from me, rucksack and blanket neatly on his back. Nothing concrete formed in my mind, just a synaptic reaction. Formless primal howling erupted from deep inside me, an alarm broadcast to the universe. My wails rolled down the hill and across the open space, through the cracks in the cabin walls, touching each fir needle and tree trunk as they filled the surrounding woods. I was wounded. Like an animal, I attacked, flinging myself off the ledge and onto Hakim's back, knocking him to the ground. He rolled up to protect himself. I went at him, flailing and screaming. In New Haven I had fled. Not this time.

"What do you think you're doing? You need to talk to me. You can't just walk away!"

Hakim lay still, trying not to aggravate me more. Carol ran up the path. She had heard everything from the main cabin. Anyone could listen. I didn't care. He was not leaving without acknowledging me. He couldn't just walk away from me like that. We were married! I did not cry and beg him to stay. I did not tell him I loved him and plead that he not do this to me. I was stunned, incoherent with shock. Most of all I wanted him to give me my due. Take that, you motherfucker! I hit him, threw myself on him, and beat him with my fists as hard as I could. Here I am. Deal with me.

Hakim righted himself, brushed away the dirt, and walked off. I was left in the dust on the path, full of tears and beyond anything crying could do. Carol, coming toward me, passed Hak as he moved away. I walked with her to my tent, sobbing out the details of what had happened.

"I saw you! You jumped on his back and pummeled him with your fists. I can hear your scream and still see you beating him up. It was such an animal response."

I sat there, unable to say much, appreciative of her support.

"At first I thought you were stung by a bee. You were all over the place.

I was stunned. Rocky or somebody pulled you off of Hak. You were really trying to beat him up."

I vaguely remembered someone intervening—but what did the facts matter? They told the story, but I was still in the story. Putting the pieces together eased each moment but the flow of feelings was too much to ingest. Unlike New Haven, this time there was no light to turn off; everything was all too clear in the bright midday sun.

I had married this man, overlooking all the terrible things he had done to me. But if there was one thing that seemed true, that seemed rock solid, it was that Hakim wanted me. He had pursued me and stuck with me. We were together, a couple, at least as best I knew how. There would be children in the future, our children, a commingling of us both, a little bit Indonesian, a little bit me, distinctly Eurasian. I knew what my baby would look like. We were one, together, past, present, and future—and now, in an instant, over and done, finished. No counseling. No "Margaret, we have a problem."

My efforts to talk with Hak, to let him know when things didn't feel right, were rarely heard. I hated it when Lev was with us on our trip west and living in our apartment in Eugene. They were the couple. The only way I could get Hak's attention was to explode. Throwing the ashtray and ripping his shirt in Eugene was not how I envisioned problem-solving with my husband, but Hak did what Hak wanted. He was tougher than me. I gave in and shut off and that was where we were, too closed off and too far gone. But it hurt.

"When you broke down and cried I felt terrible for you," Carol said. "Now that I know what happened I feel terrible for me too." Carol was my closest friend, but her needs were never far from the picture. In this case, though, she was justified, at least somewhat. We were all so close—what affected one of us affected all of us.

"You and Hak are everything. It was Clint and me and Hakim and you. Now that's lost. This is like my parents splitting up. Very scary. It could happen to me. Nothing is permanent."

She continued to try to make sense of it, reinforcing my disbelief and rage in the process.

"I had no intimation that anything like this was happening. It came out of the blue. Did you expect this?"

I shook my head.

"You mean it just happened, slam bam thank you ma'am?"

I nodded.

"I really loved that you tried to beat him up," Carol said, getting excited. "I thought it was just great. Somebody fucks you over, beat the shit out of them. I admire you for it, Margaret."

She was trying, but everything was bitter fruit.

Most of the men kept their distance for a while, letting Carol help me through my shock, woman to woman. No sides were drawn. They were men; they understood the impulse and at the same time they were friends, thrown by the loss of an important member of our group.

I knew, deep inside, that Hak did not leave for a one-night stand or an experiment in new ways of relating. He was leaving for good. For a month there was no word from him and then, on my birthday, a note was delivered via Rocky, who had been visiting Footbridge. He found me at my tent on a bright, sunny day, sitting on the edge of my platform under the shade of the trees. I took out the folded piece of paper and read the words that slammed and sealed the door shut. Kathy was pregnant. My marriage was over, and we hadn't even made it to our second anniversary. Hak took the car. He left the tent. No need for a lawyer. Property is always the easy part. It all comes down to the children. Kathy was carrying the Eurasian baby that should have been mine.

A few summers later, visiting my parents at their cabin in Vermont, I sat with my mother in a rowboat on the small lake by their property. She fished as we floated in the soft evening light. I put the oars up and started to talk, a rare moment of closeness and candor between us.

"Mom." She looked up from her fishing. "I want children. I don't care if I have a husband or not. It's the only kind of love I can trust, the only kind that will always be there, that will endure." I was asking for her support, letting her know what I thought the future might bring, but the real watershed was saying out loud to myself that I no longer trusted. If this is what I got from a husband, why open to that commitment again, to that level of supposed intimacy?

In truth, both Hakim and I participated in the failure of our relationship. Our differences caught up with us. We each brought limitations; living in a group masked them, the times an incentive to look the other way. Really loving someone was not easy for me. I knew how to wrap up an idea, but unwrapping a feeling was harder, and this relationship did not provide the safest environment in which to learn. Ultimately the truth was that I picked him, I stayed, and I married him, ignoring every road sign that pointed to danger. My difficulty with confrontation, my willingness to capitulate, and my model of intimacy were part of the mix, helping to shore up Hakim's power over me instead of containing it by challenging him or walking away. But the answer is never quite that easy, is it? I also needed Hakim, or thought I did. Walls no longer crumbled in my mind, but doors opened, and he was the man that held them for me, consistently helping me move through to the other side. He expanded my life. Could I trust myself to do the same without him? Insight, however, was a luxury that came later. Now I was alone, a woman in the woods with no man to help her. I had seen all the single women slowly disappear from our group. Survival was challenging. A few fresh converts arrived for the summer, but even they were starting to think of apartments in Eugene and friends in Hawaii. Floras Creek was man's country. Somebody in the couple had to be able to wield a chain saw, build a structure, repair a vehicle, relate to the other guys, and generally be the other half of a partnership. Alone it was hard. Considered against the eventuality of winter, it was nigh impossible. Rainy season was due in a few months.

This is my home, I thought, lying in my tent several weeks after Hak had left. Everyone, every friend I have is right here on this land. I don't want to move, certainly not back to Cleveland to live with my parents. If I leave, how would I support myself? I could hardly breathe at the thought of working inside all day, doing some stifling office task where I would have to wear high heels, stockings, and my fake chignon. Worst of all, when nine to five was over, there would be nobody—no friends, husband, or community—with whom to share my life. Lying inside my little tent alone, looking up at the sunlight and shadows on the fabric above me, it became clear. I am staying. Why would I leave? Because Hakim walked out on me? No, everything I wanted was right here. My clarity was absolute and I had full faith that I could make it work. You just put one foot in front of the other and made it happen. The hardest part, I had learned, was figuring out what I wanted. Lost in my early morning musings, I looked around, my practicality kicking in. First things first: where will I live? I'm going to need a lot more than this tent. Housing was my primary challenge.

# CHAPTER 17   With a Little Help from My Friends

THERE WAS ONLY ONE SOLUTION, and that was to build myself a cabin. But how? The guys were the architects, not me. Clint was working on a castle, at least relative to the rest of us, a homestead to please Carol. Steve Ledbetter, who had joined us from Three Rivers, was methodically building his home on the lower forty acres. Without even trying, Stuart's aesthetic channeled every recluse from the Old West in his small bachelor shanty, set amidst scrubby manzanita and huckleberry bushes. In actuality we were all building shacks worthy of depression-era photojournalism. As Hakim's natty older brother Gilang declared, somewhat aghast, when months earlier he arrived for a brief visit from Manhattan: "Hak, if you wanted to live in third-world squalor you could have stayed in Indonesia."

Gilang be damned. This land and these people were my present and future, my community and home. I belonged. What could be more powerful? I "remarried" before the bed had even cooled, transferring my loyalty and faith to a new kind of union, my group. In the past I fought change almost every step of the way, head down, bent over, backing in but moving forward. This time, on my own, with no outside pressure, I claimed my future upright.

"First," Clint instructed me, "you need to measure and mark out a grid for your foundation poles." That created a problem right there, foundation poles. Where was I going to get lumber? I was surrounded by trees but short on skills. Buying wood was too expensive. That left the beach, which offered more convenient and affordable shopping. I borrowed Stuart's truck and along with Carol and Georgia, a visiting guest, drove to the ocean. We lifted and loaded a batch of crooked driftwood logs into Stuart's truck, feeling like Amazons. Was it just a few years ago I was worrying about whether I could wear slacks instead of a skirt to work?

Clint helped me mark off my floor plan, pounding small sticks of wood into the dirt to form a square that was true. Carpentry was precise. Next he indicated the grid for the foundation poles that would support the floor joists. Joists? This was a whole new vocabulary. With this information Clint packed up his tools and left me to finish the job, which seemed manageable if I broached it one step at a time. Holes. I could do that.

I lifted our posthole digger and admired the cleverness of its design, two handles connected to two curved blades, one fulcrum in the middle for opening and closing. So simple. Everything about it spoke to the task at hand, purpose and engineering elegantly one, mechanically clear. Now that I had fully appreciated the tool, it was time to use it. I straddled a spot and grabbed the long handles in each of my fists, keeping them perpendicular to the ground. Holding tight, I jerked the rods straight up until their tops were higher than my head and on tiptoe, using the whole force of my body, rammed those sharp metal tips into the earth, slicing a circular hole, or at least the start of one. The earth was hard and dry, often requiring several stabs, up and down like a piston, to cut through the soil and its network of fibrous roots. After the jolt of impact, I reamed the handles open, pinching the harvest of loosened dirt between the half cylinder blades, and pulled out whatever soil I had collected, depositing it to the side, ready to repeat the steps again. Load by load a round hole formed, home for a sawed-off piece of driftwood that, when aligned with its brethren, geometrically formed the foundation of my new home. The simplicity was breathtaking, as was the labor.

My entire cabin was built without the aid of power tools. Even the sawhorse was handmade from small limbs I cut from surrounding trees. The only exceptions were the boards I used for flooring, siding, and studs. We scavenged those from nearby properties, cannibalizing the carrion of old cabins that had fallen in on themselves, deconstructing one structure so that it could be resurrected in another form at a new location, our place.

Once the foundation was in, it was time for framing. Everyone helped, but day-by-day it was my job to saw the wood and keep the momentum going. I had to be a force that was assisted, not a charity case that was carried. The drudgework was mine.

Clint and Stuart cut down slim young trees and used the trunks as studs for framing the walls. My home was starting to take shape, a basic cube with a slanted shed roof. I spent the next week pulling nails out of recycled boards. Clint put in headers to support the windows and doors. Now it was time to close in the structure. I measured and hand cut the salvaged boards, nailing them to the saplings and two by fours that outlined my home. This was something I could do by myself. I did need some help building a ladder to reach the top of my cabin. Clint cut down two saplings and showed me how to firmly nail branches between the poles. I wanted to make sure this was built safely.

*Margaret's cabin at Floras Creek*

It took me over a year to build my cabin, with time off for the rainy season. By the second summer I was ready for the final step, weatherproofing. Sealing my cabin in tarpaper was like Christo wrapping the Reichstag. This was more than a building; it was art. I had made a statement, a phoenix rising out of the ashes.

I loved my cabin. In actuality it was a fifteen-by-fifteen-foot tar-paper shack. There was no adornment, just black wrapping broken by a few salvaged windows with peeling paint and mismatched, weathered frames. But everything about it was mine. My will, my labor, and my imagination made it happen, every step a challenge and an investment. This was my baby. The most beautiful home I ever had.

Pride of place in my cabin was reserved for the insides of an old woodstove. This unadorned firebox, ravenously burning my hard-won stash of hand-split firewood, served two purposes. I could heat water on top for a cup of tea or a sponge bath, and it was also my hearth, the only source of warmth to make things snug in the winter. Even though it was small, my home felt roomy. By making the sleeping loft a second story, the entire downstairs was left open. For coziness, I covered my bed with a thick Greek fleece of sheep's wool and a striped Guatemalan blanket, both vestigial remnants from my wedding. I built a ladder of two-by-fours cut to fit between the interior studs, a straight up and down climb, to reach the loft. The topmost step served as a nightstand on which I placed my flashlight and glasses. Without streetlights it got very dark, a problem at night when I had to climb down to find the can reserved for peeing, the closest thing I had to indoor plumbing. During the day, outdoor plumbing in the soft loam of the forest defined my little piece of heaven. All I had to do was find a spot away from my cabin, dig through the layer of rotting leaves with a back swipe of my boot, drop trou, and squat. Like a dog, I covered my business and moved on. We had the luxury of space and isolation to make it possible, and the great outdoors was certainly better than a smelly outhouse.

In addition to the ladder, I fit two-by-fours between the wall studs to form shelves for my small collection of possessions: a toothbrush, a few books, and my ever-present netsukes. Bit by bit they seemed out of place. The textured and variegated bark on the poles that framed my cabin was decoration enough. No dry wall or insulation hid them from view. Lacy wisps of delicate green moss still hung from their sides. Outside was now inside, each echoing the other. My only piece of furniture was my stool, a stump rescued from the woodpile. The stubby base of a branch protruded from one side, forming a very convenient handle for moving it closer or farther from the firebox, a rudimentary sort of thermostat that worked in conjunction with the amount of fuel that fed the blaze. Therein lay the rub, or at least the chop. If I was going to stay warm, I'd need to lay in a supply of wood, quartered, stacked, and covered, ready for the cold and rain of winter. I could saw and chop but I knew I needed help getting logs. We had moved past the romance and labor of two-man whipsaws to a gasoline-powered, chain-driven, phallic behemoth whining through the woods fueling our life style. Like most of our big tools, it was for the men, too heavy for me to wield safely. Once again, Clint, the owner of our big chainsaw, was very helpful. He cut trees and fallen wood into manageable pieces for me. My job was to haul them up to my cabin and split them into quarters.

Outside my cabin was a large round of fir about knee high, my chopping block, an essential part of each homestead. Scattered at its base were smaller rounds. I picked one up and placed it on the rough surface of my block. Then I reached for my axe, letting it hang down from my hand, the weight of the iron tugging on my arm, its heft a satisfying force. I lifted the metal head and carefully balanced the blade on the center of the round. With both arms outstretched, right hand front, I gripped the handle and measured out my distance, legs wide in preparation for the swing. Now I was ready. A slight halt as I focused my intention, a moment too small to measure but enough to heighten my awareness and set me on edge. I felt a force gather within me and then it burst forth, set in motion as I moved my weight back into my right foot and started the swing, sweeping the axe by my boot, the weight of the head pulling down and out. All this was to gain momentum for the upward swoop, the rebound that threw the axe bouncing high over my head, my shoulder pulled open with a pleasing ache, my forward arm sliding upwards ready to guide it all home. Poised like an Olympic diver, I was caught, extended in the brief moment before descent, the axe hovering at the top of its arc where my swing and gravity joined to bring the blade crashing down. With a crack the round cleaved, each severed half flying in opposite directions. The movement was fluid. I was one with the axe, feeling the snap of the wood throughout my entire body. Neat and sweet. Thwack. The blade made the cut and found its home, stuck at a jaunty angle in the stump. I jerked the axe free and picked up one of the fallen halves, placing it on the chopping block. Thwack, once more, and the wood was in quarters, split along the grain; fresh, clean and fragrant, so neat, so satisfying. I knew where my fuel came from and where it was going. My body made it happen.

That winter I flew to Cleveland, visiting my parents on my own stolen airline ticket. To my surprise I was stifled in their centrally heated house, where no undercurrent of breezes filtered in through cracks to freshen the enclosed air. Their rugs, paintings, and seemingly endless collection of things overwhelmed my senses, which sought out the simplicity of my cabin. I knew I was clunky and rough in my heavy boots and oversized, over-washed sweater. But most of all I felt out of place because I was full of physical energy that needed to be released, confined in a space that was too well sealed. I needed to move to the rhythm of chopping wood, craving the sound, smell, and sensation of splitting rounds of fir, feeling my body swell and sing with the synchronized movement until I was warm through and through.

# CHAPTER 18  Me and Bobby McGee

AS A GROUP WE WERE EVERYTHING TO EACH OTHER, but I was still alone, single, without a partner. About a year after Hak left, my eye landed on Stuart, but very lightly, some tender wounds still open. He was handsome, helpful, and available. As I struggled to finish my cabin, Stuart was always there to help, gently encouraging and actively hammering. I had never seen Stuart with a girlfriend, even in New Haven. His one true love was Molly, his gentle German shepherd, rescued from the pound in Colorado along with her brother Ralph. There was no hiding, though, that he'd been a bit of a rake and a ramblin' man, a high school football hero and an Air Force playboy, clearly at home with a pool cue in his hand.

Our neighborhood pleasure palace was Stormy's, a lone concrete bunker with a high horizontal strip of windows, set off from the coast highway by a deep parking lot of gravel. Day or night there was always at least one dusty battered truck parked at a random angle, letting the community know as they drove by that its owner was inside enjoying a little respite. To this Mecca flocked every alcoholic, aging single and would-be cowboy living in the surrounding hills, us included. There were always a scattering of geezers and geezerettes at the bar, all of them just as achingly vulnerable in their optimism and need for community as we were. Around the pool table was where the real testosterone flowed; younger, competitive, and slightly inebriated challengers threw down the gauntlet with quarters on the table's rim. Stuart, his drugstore cowboy blood running strong, was at home. For the rest of us it was foreign travel. We were titillated by the new and hoped to blend in. There was a jukebox and a grill behind the counter, but this was definitely not a dinner and dancing establishment.

Stormy, the eponymous owner, liked to philosophize, frequently summing up his observations with "Same ball of wax wherever you go," while resting his arms on the bar and contemplatively looking out into mid-distance. This, his signature sentence, signaled the close of the conversation, but it always left hanging the question of just where he had been, with no intimation that it was much farther than a few counties over. We, however, were the world and had landed right on his doorstep. There was never any hostility directed at us, just interest. Everyone knew from television that "hippie" meant naked bodies, wild sex, and illegal drugs, and here we were, bellied up to the bar in their own backyard. We in turn were equally entranced with our own myths about them, an entertaining stand-off.

Looking for a little town time, five of us bundled up and rode in the back of Stuart's truck to Stormy's. The evening was pretty typical—some beer, some chat, people watched us, we watched them, each of us a reality show for the other. Stuart stood at the pool table, quietly and steadily sipping his scotch, moving his way in and out of the competition. There was a lull and he came over to the booth, encouraging me to put my quarter down and try the game. We played a little. Stuart was a patient teacher, a time-honored courtship ritual, but I could feel pressure building from the real players, discreet but restive, waiting in the shadows to get back to the table. Several drinks and a few games later, we clambered back into the truck. I got to sit inside on the ride up the mountain.

When we got home, it was dark and Stuart offered to walk me back to my cabin. By the time we reached my clearing, I knew he would stay. With only one stump stool for furniture, the only place to settle was my loft, a small platform with just enough room for a double-sized foam mattress and my sleeping bag. The shed roof of my cabin slanted from the top of the mismatched row of windows at the head of my bed to the opposite wall, forming a cozy wedge for sleeping. A kerosene lantern sat on the sill above my pillows. I struck a match, slipping it under the glass chimney to light the wick. Now we could see each other in the gentle light of the flame. Stuart followed me up, but hesitated a moment as he sat at the edge of the loft.

"I can't help thinking that you are still Hakim's."

"Stuart, he's gone. They have a baby together."

"I always thought Hak was so lucky. I liked you all that time in New Haven."

"You did? I never knew that." I was truly surprised. "But it's over, Stuart. He left me."

Stuart eased down and lay facing me, his voice soft. "I used to wish that this could happen." Clearly I had entered a new reality. Not just one in which Stuart was lying on my previously connubial sleeping bag, but a world where I had been the star, totally unbeknownst to me. In Stuart's mind there was a place ready and waiting for me. Both of us were a little stunned to find ourselves together in what before had been his private fantasy. I made the transition easily, savoring this Texas cowboy. Stuart was big and solid, familiar and comforting, a man who knew how to live in the woods, almost the Roy Rogers of my prepubescent fantasies, just less the hero type and not quite as sober.

Moving carefully, Stuart raised himself up until I was under him and then sat back on his haunches, straddling me, his head brushing against the bare weathered boards of my ceiling. He looked at me in the soft light and held the moment, his voice gentle and open. "This is for you," he said. One little sentence, so very simple, but it filled my mossy home. I lay still, feeling his intent around me. I was being offered a gift, the present of being given to, and finally it was right.

Stuart left in the early morning to return to his shack, both of us feeling very sweet but quite confused. It had been Clint and Carol and Hak and Margaret for several years. Stuart was right. Hakim and I were still a couple, our shared mutual history part of our tribe's identity as well as our own. Taking someone in requires time, adjusting as they fill the nooks and crannies of your essence and you each ease around the other's ways, slowly building a mutual history and pattern of being. Bleeding someone out also takes awhile, the trickle leaving empty spaces in danger of collapse. I was reeling from being left, shoring myself up as best I could while gradually filling the void. There was a lot of hurt and scar tissue that needed to be massaged away. But I was smitten. That Stuart sure was sweet. We circled each other, keeping our distance after our interlude in the dark but connected in some very tender way, me, unsteady and vulnerable, protecting my fragile self, Stuart fighting his own battles and not just with Hakim.

Stuart had a fissure inside him where he could disappear, especially after a few drinks. He usually drank at night, unobtrusively but with a slow and steady hand. The day we went to the beach took us all by surprise, an end-of-summer, warm afternoon that was reason enough, in and of itself, to celebrate. We filled Stuart's truck and headed down the hill with no plans for anything more than a few hours of sun and frolicking by the waves. Once we got there, Clint and Georgia went off for a walk. Everyone mixed and recombined as the afternoon wore on. Carol sought me out and we walked by the waves. She was fretting over Clint and Georgia, feeling, rightly so, that something was in the air. As we talked, I noticed Stuart in the distance, walking along the sand by the hills that formed a buffer between the beach and the highway. My radar was up. His head was down and he seemed perturbed, muttering to himself as he strode very deliberately toward the path to the parking area. I watched as Stuart opened the door to his truck, got in, and drove off, heading north on the highway toward home. Word traveled fast.

"Stuart left?"

"He'll be back."

"Maybe he just went to Stormy's."

"He would never leave us here."

"Hope he gets back in time for dinner."

Everyone had an idea, but no one was worried. We always looked out for each other. Odd behavior was just that, we took it in stride, tolerance greasing our wheels on a daily basis. The afternoon wore on, coming to the point where we could feel the day, as well as our interest, cooling, going home an appealing thought. Individually we scanned the roadway, hoping to catch sight of Stuart's truck. Collectively we sat around voicing concern and annoyance, a low disgruntled undercurrent in the air. This was no longer funny.

"Look, I've got Kokia, he's hungry." Katrina was fed up. "What am I supposed to do?" She, the ultimate responsible mother, could not protect her child. Who were the children here?

"He couldn't just leave us. Maybe he got in an accident."

Rocky volunteered to hitchhike home and bring back another vehicle. "But," he noted, "Stuart will probably be back before me."

We all agreed that it wasn't worth doing and continued to wait, resigned to our temporary fate. Clint and Paul went to look for driftwood and started a fire, our summer shirts and light jackets inadequate protection from the chill that was coming off the ocean. Our hope disappeared with the setting of the sun. The mood blackened. An acrid undercurrent of resentment soured everything as we huddled together for warmth, dozing on and off through the night, waves continually crashing in the background. We were stuck and Stuart was the cause.

From time to time complaints erupted. "I'm freezing!" "I'm starving!" "This is miserable!" "How much longer 'til daylight?" Even, "Do you think something happened to him?" But never, "What a stupid drunken asshole." No, he was one of ours, this was a group marriage. We overlooked our partners' flaws as long as we could. What we needed to do was get through the night and send out some hitchhikers in the morning so they could drive back and bring us all home.

When the sun rose, Rocky and Paul trudged through the sand and up the hill, putting out their thumbs in the hope of a ride north. A truck appeared speeding down the opposite side of the two-lane highway and looking familiar. Stuart. He screeched across both lanes of the highway. From the beach we could see him pick up Rocky and Paul. Then he U-turned again and pulled into the parking area a few more yards down the road. We gathered around him, frustrated, our anger put away but not totally out of sight. A toke can only do so much.

"What happened?

"Where were you?"

"We were freezing here all night."

Stuart was chagrined. "I don't know."

"What do you mean you don't know?

"I think I went to Stormy's." Stuart looked as confused as the rest of us. "This morning I woke up in my cabin with my clothes on. The first thing that hit me was the beach. I jumped in my truck and tore down here as fast as I could."

There was nothing more to say, on his part or ours; we all knew what had happened, but no one wanted to say it out loud. Substance abuse was a term that came later, for another generation, when twelve-step programs became ubiquitous. Now our mantra was expanding and including, making room for differences without rancor or judgment. Drinking, drugs, they were all mind expanding, even as we reluctantly began to feel the disarray that lay in their dark side. Our ride back home was quiet.

Feelings tempered and things settled back into their normal rhythm, which for Stuart and I became the dance of the damaged, our own personal two-step. I healed and hoped. He drank and detached. As a Texan, a football hero, an artist, and a recluse, I thought I had found in Stuart the opposite of Hakim. I had, but that was the problem; both angles of repose were extreme, each a reflection of the other. Our one time together was the extent of our relationship, at least the realized part.

At the end of each day I walked down to the cabin for dinner, looking for food, company, and Stuart, who sipped his way through the tasks and conviviality of the evening, a bit in the background, separate, looking in from the edge. His drinking was so quiet and unobtrusive, the coffee cup of wine or whisky such an extension of himself, that its effects tiptoed up on us even as they were dependable in their regularity. Stuart, not a happy drunk, withdrew first into silence and then deep into his own darkness. I knew because my radar was attuned to his presence, hoping he would walk me back to my cabin one more time. While I silently longed, Stuart slowly receded, disappearing inside himself and ultimately out the door, painfully mining his own bitter ore.

# CHAPTER 19   Sgt. Pepper's Lonely Hearts Club Band

MY LITTLE HOME WAS COZY AT NIGHT. Darkness came early and was all encompassing. Friends, settled in their own cabins, were scattered in the woods around me. Snug, I lit a fire. A chipped, white enamel basin, rescued from an abandoned shack, hung from a nail to the right of my door. I filled it with water carried from the main cabin in an empty plastic milk jug and put it on the stove to heat, waiting patiently on my stump stool while it warmed. Bit by bit I fed small pieces of wood into the firebox, peaceful and dreamy as I lost myself in the meditative dance of the flames. My plan was to soap my legs so that I could shave them smooth in the privacy of my woodsy home, just me, no other eyes or judgments, alone with my thoughts, lost in the ritual. I knew this was not politically correct, that we were all human animals and should revel in the glory of our bodies. Every day I publicly espoused that stance, but hey, those other women had legs that were pretty close to hairless. My legs were one of my best features, but they were hairy. I could live with furry underarms. No deodorant. No problem, but I needed my legs. Shapely and firm, they made me feel pretty. Sitting by my firebox, lit only by the light of my kerosene lantern, I reached for the sliver of hard, white soap that rested in the curve of a leathery leaf, my makeshift soap dish. Using just a little water, I lathered first one leg and then the other; deliberately pulling my razor along each calf and thigh, scraping them clean with repeated upward sweeps, every stroke clearing a ribbon of fresh silky skin. Done, I carefully wiped away any soapy reside with a damp cloth, everything dark and still around me, my legs shiny in their smoothness, content just to be.

After sitting for a bit in the silence, I reached for my battery-operated radio, dialing through static until a station from a nameless place in the Midwest came in clear. The program was a club, the Internet before cyberspace. People from all over the country called in and talked to each other. Pretty soon Betty from Alabama was playing us listeners a tune on her piano. John in Wyoming called to tell about his wife's illness. From Wisconsin, Helen replied, sending prayers for the speedy recovery of John's wife. Hazel, floating in from another isolated spot in the night, read a poem she wrote, and on and on it went, a moderator welcoming each offering, opening the door for each of us to the other. In the kerosene light of my cabin I found a community of lonely souls seeking each other over the airwaves. What a bunch of nuts, I thought. Can you believe this? And there I sat, rooted to my stump, listening along in my dimly lit cabin with my lovely shaved legs.

Sometimes my loft felt empty. I had been married and was used to Hakim's warm body next to mine. We had brought a cat, Blacky, with us when we moved from the farm. She frequently followed me to my cabin at night, hoping for a spot near the firebox. As the stove cooled and I read, Blacky would softly steal up to my loft and lay down beside me on the shaggy Greek rug I used to cover myself. That was the cue for me to lift the edge of the heavy wool blanket and let her settle in, the curve of her spine toward me, her paws and head facing away. Blowing out the lantern, I mirrored her, turning on my side, ready for sleep. There we lay, back to back, just like a Hak and me, Blacky definitely a lot smaller and definitely of another species, yet still comforting, helping me feel less alone with that echo of a partner in my bed.

Like everyone else's homes at Floras Creek, my cozy, tar-paper shack was tucked away, no neighbors in sight. The main cabin was a five- or six-minute walk over low-growing grasses, through the surrounding woods, down the path, and into the clearing below. One winter night, like so many others, it was time to head out for the evening meal. Something, as usual, was coming down from the sky, more like a gentle mist than rain. Clouds obscured any sliver of a moon that might have been out. As I bundled up, I debated about taking a flashlight. Batteries were expensive. This was a familiar path, one I navigated every day. I knew the route and of course the lit windows of the cabin would show me the way once I got past the trees that screened my clearing. No, I can do this without a light. Throwing on a heavy sweater and a thin slicker, I tamped down the fire in my woodstove and followed my heart outside toward the warmth of good company and hot food. The night seemed darker than usual. I moved forward, instinct and memory guiding my way, but something was strange. My eyes were not adapting. Open or closed it made no difference; the view was the same, just blackness, not even a rough outline of the tall bushes that surrounded me. No problem, I thought. If I keep heading in the right direction, I'll find the path. Confident, but not as confident as before, I continued to move forward, trusting my sense of direction, feeling my way one deliberate step at a time until I bumped against a wall of wet leaves and rough branches. Reality hit. I hadn't been able to see the tall hedge of wild rhododendrons, inches in front of me, into which I had just walked. Maybe it was time to retreat and forgo dinner. I turned around, orienting toward my cabin, and looked for its outline. Gone! There wasn't the slightest shadow of dark against the blackness all around. Like a conjuror's trick, no matter how hard I peered or craned my neck, my cabin had disappeared. This was real trouble. I had no way forward and I couldn't go back.

"Help," I yelled, "help," hoping my calls were aimed in the right direction. "Stuart, Clint, help!"

The wet air hung like a baffle, soundproofing the night. What was I going to do? Night fell early. Almost twelve hours remained before daylight, long, cold, sleepless hours with nothing to protect me or help me pass the time, not even a place to lie down except the drenched ground. Despair set in. Twelve hours? No blanket, no radio, no company, no sleep. This is going to be a very long night. I was already chilled. With that awareness I knew I had bigger challenges than boredom and discomfort ahead of me. Hypothermia was a real risk. I could die of exposure. No one would think to look for me. All my friends, everyone in my immediate world, would think I decided to skip dinner. Ten minutes ago I was safe and cozy. Now I was facing death. I tried to regain control of my thoughts. What's that quote, "We have nothing to fear but fear itself?" OK, I've got it. I can do this. What a stupid way to die.

I mustered my wits and like a blind man without a cane, tentatively moved forward. Within six steps, my feet rammed against a boulder as tall as my thigh, causing me to lurch and grab for balance. Running my hands over its velvety moss brought a glimmer of recognition. I knew this rock. Every day I passed it to the right of the path that led from my clearing, through the woods, and down to the main cabin. Bent over, sliding my hands across its surface, I moved one sideways step to the left at a time, patting the rock and then the wall of adjacent bushes with little staccato movements, always keeping in touch, dependent on my fingers to read the Braille of my surroundings. When the brush abruptly ended, I stumbled forward, slightly off balance, unprepared for emptiness. Then I straightened myself, inching into the void, keeping contact with the lifeline of rhododendron with my right hand. Anchored, I flapped my left arm, reaching for anything that might give me a clue. Nothing there. Nothing? But that's it! I was at the break in the undergrowth where the path began. I entered the opening, shuffling my feet along the tamped earth, continuing to scan ahead with my extended left hand, knowing this was a short stretch. Within a few minutes the wall of saplings and undergrowth thinned, revealing the central clearing. In the distance I could see the windows of the main cabin, yellow from the lanterns, testimony to the warm tableau within. I cried, full of relief at being safe, still scared from feeling so alone. Keeping my beacon in sight, I made my way along the path as quickly as I could, looking forward to going in out of the cold.

# CHAPTER 20   Do the Loco-Motion

AT NIGHT I WAS ALONE, but by day we traveled in clusters, sharing gas and rides whenever possible. Vehicles were more complex. Our unspoken rule was that all cars and trucks could be communally used, but only with permission by the owner, somewhat of an oxymoron. In practice, the asker knew there were some people it was best not to approach and the bestower was aware there were some people it was best not to trust. We may have valued community, but private possession kept us running, transportation being too important to leave to the common good.

Individually owned cars meant individually maintained cars, a helpful survival technique that served us personally and collectively. If the wheels were yours, you took care of them, getting help if necessary. Responsibility rested with you, not an insignificant fact as community tasks often went undone, victim of the not-my-job, someone-else-will-do-it syndrome. If, out of frustration or a sense of responsibility, you did step up to a task, it was now your job, the silent, barely conscious sigh of relief from those who held back almost palpable.

When Hakim and I split, there was no formal division of property, no divorce lawyers or mediators pitting us against each other to see who got what. Actually there was precious little to fight over. After the initial blow-up, we just fizzled out and went our own ways, not even bothering to get a legal divorce until years later. In the process of separating, Hakim got our van. Evidently, driving off in our mutually owned vehicle made it his. I never thought to contest this arrangement. After all, he bought it by trading in his BMW. When we met, I didn't even know how to drive. Hakim taught me in preparation for our trip west.

Once I committed to staying and building my cabin, it became clear that I needed a vehicle. I started by borrowing. All I had to do was ask, contribute to the communal good at a different juncture of need, and the cosmic karmic scale was balanced, or at least that was my functioning reality, though I was aware that I needed to be careful not to lean too hard on any one person. Clint's truck might be best, but perhaps this time it would be good to ask Stuart. Supportive, amused, and in the spirit of the times, Stuart lent me his old Ford half-ton to haul wood through a back approach to my homestead. The venture was successful and now it was time to return the truck. My site was surrounded by leafy alders of all sizes with no road running through them, just more or less room between the trees. I eased my foot off the clutch and gently pressed on the gas pedal. Every few feet new obstacles appeared. I turned left to avoid one sapling and then swiftly twisted the steering wheel right, skirting new branches as I inched forward. Trying to drive through this leafy growth was like an organic version of bumper-cars, all my senses engaged as I sought to find a safe right of way. There was no going back and the thought of asking for help did not occur to me. I was a *Ms.*, not a *Miss.*

I crept forward until I heard a loud pop, a sharp bang that reverberated through the woods. Stuart's truck lurched to a halt and the glove compartment with the broken latch flopped open, spewing its contents. Everything was silent except for the twittering of a few birds. Leaves stuck through my open window and poked through the rim of the steering wheel. When I reached for the interior door handle and pulled up, it spun freely in its socket, no resistance, no catch, and no chance of exit. I gathered up my torso, ready to heave it against the door, something we often had to do with our ramshackle fleet of vehicles. A few thuds and I gave up. Thwarted, I reached out the window and patted my hand against the side of the truck, trying to locate the exterior handle. Maybe it still worked. It didn't. Pushing aside the invasive branches, I stuck my head out. A tree stump, about three feet high, pressed tightly against the driver side door. Carefully, I withdrew and sat back down, slowly absorbing the fact that what had been convex was now concave.

Now what? The passenger door opened, but not far enough to accommodate my body. Instead I slid feet first out the window, carefully avoiding any branches that might snag me. After slithering to freedom, I headed down the hill on foot, much less cocky than an hour ago when I was primed and ready to build, feeling less like a *Ms.* and more like a cross between Lucille Ball and a recalcitrant teenager. Everyone was outside as I approached the main cabin, alerted by the bang that echoed through the woods. No one missed that noise, the clarion call of drama, entertainment in a world without media. We could have been an African village or a medieval hamlet; something new augured excitement, everything was everyone's business. Stuart and five or six others were standing around, well aware of what had happened even before I appeared. They expectantly awaited my arrival from stage right through the trees, an audience deliciously poised in anticipation of the denouement starring me in a role I did not relish. With relief I sensed their mood, scanning for the anger that wasn't there.

"The truck is stuck," I started to explain as I moved toward everyone.

"No shit. I am sure everyone this side of the mountain heard that noise." Much laughter followed this remark, and some poking of elbows.

"Need a taxi?" Carol said, enjoying the drama.

"What do you think, Stuart? Anything left to salvage?" from another wise guy.

"Don't worry. It'll look nice up there."

"A truck rusting in the weeds is considered a lawn ornament in this neck of the woods."

Stuart stood silent, unruffled, slightly amused. His response was the one that mattered. In the end, it was his truck. When things settled, Stuart took his turn. "Let's take a look and see if there's something we can do." I knew the "we" was he and was very grateful for his acceptance and willingness to help.

Stuart savored playing the understated protagonist as he walked with me, surveying the situation and disengaging the truck with ease, hardly containing his amusement as I sat embarrassed and worried next to him on the drive back down. Ultimately he hammered out the door while I helped by holding a few tools, paying my dues in attentive concern, witness to my dependence.

The time had arrived to buy my own vehicle. I heard about an old bachelor farmer, Ed, who had a truck that had been left for years to weather in the grass behind his ramshackle cabin. Clint drove me to Ed's little homestead, where the 1945 Chevy was up to its running board in weeds, the blue paint powdery with dirt and age, its tires too flat to inspire any thoughts of motion. But my, oh my, its lines were beautiful. Like Cinderella trying on the prince's slipper, I knew it fit just right. Here was my baby.

"One hundred dollars," Ed said, "as is."

"Does it run?"

"Used to."

"Clint?"

"I don't know," he replied. "Pretty old, but some of these trucks last forever. I guess we should see if it starts."

*Margaret and her truck at Floras Creek*

I hovered around, once again appreciatively clucking, while Clint fiddled and finagled, working his mechanical magic. Sputters and putts focused our hopeful attention as the patient came to life, but then expired once again. More tinkering, some automotive farting, and then, like Toad in *Wind in the Willows*, I had a viable vehicle, or at least I did once we found some old tires in the weeds and resurrected a couple still on the truck.

As an investment, this one was a bit risky. Would the truck continue to run or would one of its classic but elderly parts fail, leaving me with stuck gears or a non-combustible engine, both far beyond my skills or my pocket book to remedy? One hundred dollars was it, all that I had. Clint looked at me. I looked back, trying to divine some profound knowledge that would assure me I was making the right choice. Ultimately I had to look into myself to claim the answer.

"I'm going for it," I said. I paid Ed in cash, leaving him hoe in hand in the middle of his dusty potato patch.

Clint started his own engine. After a few adjustments with the manual choke I followed suit, pulling out and leading the way, flatulently pooting out puffs of white smoke behind me.

Once we arrived at Floras Creek, it was time to look a little more closely. Clint patiently gave me a crash course in automotive mechanics. My truck was a textbook in the basics of the internal combustion engine; everything was there, logical and easily accessible. The sparks fired, pressure built up in the cylinders, the cams moved, motion was translated, and I had trans-portation. Adjusting the timing was a bit tricky. What was really fun was setting the tolerance on the valve lifts. This was done by slipping a thin, three-inch-long sliver of precisely calibrated metal between each cylinder and its valve. Preset standards needed to be met and all the tolerances had to match. Like an initiate in a secret fraternity I was learning a whole new language, and the tools were to die for. Fanning out the splay of stain-less steel blades, each graded into minutely different thicknesses, was an obsessive's delight. Each implement was a revelation, pure in how well it fit its one specific job. My toolbox was a jewel box, full of mechanical treasures, beautiful in their design and functionality. Doors opened and I walked through. That was the thrill of it all. Now I was set. I had my house and my truck, time to settle into the routines and challenges of our not so everyday existence.

# CHAPTER 21   Everyday People

BEFORE WE DROPPED OUT, FOOD SHOPPING WAS EASY. We marched up and down brightly stocked aisles, gluttonously feeding the carts in front of our stomachs with the excess of our culture; our jobs, our parents, or our scholarships covered the costs at check-out. At Greenleaf we learned to forage and farm, but food stamps continued to be an important source of sustenance, supplemented by tax refunds and unemployment. Over time these lingering sources of income dwindled, forcing us to be more resourceful. In this frame of mind we discovered a new source of bounty, a place where opportunity knocked, the back door, home of the halt, the lame, the rotten, and the outdated, not pretty, but within our budget.

Two big dumpsters sat against the fence behind the grocery store, their lids partially ajar, unable to close over the rising jumble of smashed corrugated boxes, stale baked goods, culled produce, and outdated containers—a gleaner's paradise, free for our taking. We descended like feral animals, stooped and scurrying, careful to avoid the birds that swooped to compete for the territory. One of us held the dumpster open while the rest took turns standing on a plastic milk crate, bent over the trash, pawing through the pile to look for bonanzas. A list was a luxury; we got what was given, different every time, yielding to the flow of dumpster karma, an extension of our way of life. Underneath slit boxes and spilled detergent we might find lettuce, not tight bleached-out heads but the unruly outer leaves carefully removed to please misguided shoppers. We were doing America a favor, clearing away their trash, which was now our treasure. Cottage cheese with a close expiration date was a delicacy as long as the weather was cold. Brown bananas were great for baking and soft tomatoes still tasty as long as they weren't moldy. Clad in our secondhand clothes, also previously discarded, we looked as scruffy as the produce we found, the boundary between what was culled and who was doing it somewhat blurred. Then, with our truck filled, or not, depending on our luck that day, we headed back home, Grendel hauling his bounty back to his lair, outcast marauders after a day's work, quite pleased with our initiative.

In addition to hunting there was gathering. At home, where our well-worn attire blended in with the natural world, a dusting of dirt and con-

stant decay being the realities of forest living, we discovered the plenti-
tude at our feet that grew wild for the picking.

At dinner, over a salad of ruffled dumpster greens, Paul offered an even
more economical possibility. "Shorty told me we can find miner's lettuce
up here," he said, drizzling a little more olive oil from the tin his family had
sent, pressed from their trees in Greece.

"What's that?" I asked. I had read Ewell Gibbons, the wild food guru,
and was alert to the romance of foraging. Why pass up an opportunity to
move even further back through evolution? Like I said, we were nothing if
not high-achieving and competitive. We could do without, better than the
best of them, or at least we were going to give it a good try.

"A wild green," Paul replied, after clearing his palate with a swig of orange juice from an outdated container.

The next morning I explored near my cabin. When I looked carefully, I
could see little leaves that fit the plant's description.

"Totally free!" was Carol's ecstatic response as we prepared dinner that
night.

"Make sure you wash it well," Stuart cautioned. "You know—slugs!"

"I'm not eating any dinner with slugs," squealed Kokia.

Katrina calmed him, did a double-check, and the meal moved on, all
of us one step closer to the land and further from everything we used to
know.

Scavenging society's leftovers and nature's surprises were not enough.
We needed a garden. Clint lovingly resurrected an ancient bulldozer that
clunked on lumbering tracks, rhythmically put-putting as it moved back
and forth, plowing the dirt in our designated garden spot. As he finished
one more turn in the clearing, a little uphill from the main cabin, his
homemade tractor stalled. Clint got out, folded back the engine cover,
and bent over, his arms extended deep into the motor's innards, where
he tinkered and twisted, jiggled and torqued, making some adjustments
to bring it back to life. Clint withdrew his hands. They were covered with
a mixture of oil, dirt, and a little blood from some scrapes. Clint grabbed
a towel hung out on the clothesline by the cabin, not just any towel, but a
clean one, painstakingly hand-scrubbed by Katrina, in water she pumped
at the sink and heated on the woodstove. Kokia, Katrina's diminutive alter

*Stuart unloading wood, Floras Creek*

ego, sat on the stoop, dumbfounded and offended, watching as the white cloth was unthinkingly desecrated, silent witness to the complex undercurrents among us. What was a simple reflex to Clint was an afternoon's work to Katrina.

Once Clint finished turning the soil, we needed to enrich it for planting. Our haphazard compost pile, more a garbage heap with dirt, was a start, but it would take a while to mature. We had fresh chicken droppings, a rich source of nutrients for the soil, but they were too strong to be applied directly, a concern that ultimately became a moot point. After great debates about whether the chickens should have free will or not, we built a large fenced enclosure to contain them; that is, until the cost of feed became prohibitive. Ultimately we let them loose to forage for themselves, leaving us free to forage for their eggs. No one formally decided on this two-step solution. Like most things, it just happened as everyone tired of the debate and someone took initiative, usually one of the men. Once a direction was set in motion others followed, all of us relieved by the opportunity to take action.

If you could make it happen, you had power, a method of planning and hierarchy that certainly left us women at a big disadvantage. As we abandoned modern technology, daily becoming more dependent on the sheer physical strength and outdoor skills of the men for survival, our voices and choices diminished to pre-liberation levels, with a risk of sliding so far backward we could lose the vote. Suffragettes, after all, did emanate from an urban base. Carol, however, saw her chance. We all had our talents. She could initiate in her own way. Our garden plot, a field of nutrient-starved clods, needed organic amendments to transform it into soft chocolatey loam. My birthday was approaching, creating a confluence of events too good to pass up, especially as the garden was still my special field of interest. She enlisted help, theatre always necessitating both a producer and a crew.

The morning of my birthday was quiet, a day like every other day. It was mid-July, hot, and I wanted to work the soil, still hopeful that we could grow vegetables, even if we had missed spring planting. No one else was around. I assumed they were either working on their cabins or having a lazy morning. In the background I could hear a vehicle straining up the hill in low gear. Slowly it came into view. I didn't recognize the truck but could see Clint, Stuart, and Carol in the cab, heads bobbing as they bounced across the uneven ground. Strangely the truck did not stop at the cabin but continued to climb up the rise toward me and then right across the roughly tilled dirt.

"Hey, where are you going?" I called out, protective of my turf.

I waited as the truck slowed and came to a stop about ten feet from where I stood, a rather pungent odor starting to make itself known.

"Whose truck?" I asked, "and why did you park it here, right where I'm trying to garden?" I was still a bit indignant.

They climbed out of the cab. Carol, taking the lead, moved ahead of Clint and Stuart and struck a pose, hands clasped under her chin, eyes rolled heavenward. Standing there, hoe in hand, I waited. Timing is everything. Carol, now fully established center stage and engaged with her audience, broke into song. "Happy birthday to you, Happy birthday to you, Happy birthday, dear Margaret, Happy birthday to you."

I still did not get it.

Realizing her performance failed to bring dénouement to the drama, Carol took a more direct approach. "Look! It's your present," she said, flinging her arms wide and gesturing with a twist of her body behind her. I stood there, quizzical, uncomprehending. More was needed. Carol, full of anticipation, obliged, taking me by the arm, leading me around to the back of the spattered one-ton farm truck while Stuart and Clint followed. "Ta da!" she said with a big smile as we arrived at the rank rear end, fully loaded with a mound of muck, brown slimy hay poking through the side slats. Clint let down the tailgate with a clunk, which cued Carol once again. "Happy Birthday!" she cried.

I stared at the reeking load in front of me, the reality slowing dawning that this dark, moist pile of cow shit, looming chest high, was mine. Fertilizer for my garden. No ribbon, no wrapping, no gift card or receipt, just a truck load of partially rotted excrement, redolent of the barnyard and oozing love, their thrill with the sublime and the ridiculous as much a part of the offering as the mountain of manure itself.

"Thank you," I said, dropping my hoe to give Carol a big hug.

"It was a shit load of work," offered Clint, smiling.

"No shit!" said Stuart.

I could not stop grinning, even as I helped shovel out the truck.

We got everything plowed and planted, but access to water, a critical element in gardening, presented a problem. Oregon summers were dry. Inside, for daily domestic use, we had the convenience of our black iron hand pump. Outside, Clint installed a temperamental gas pump by the well that was never able to consistently pull enough water, force it uphill and through our jerry-rigged irrigation system to make the garden grow. The motor constantly needed Clint's mechanical magic. I, as the one doing the gardening, was left to ineffectually follow his instructions that continually, for me, came up dry.

Our next approach was a water tank that we hoped, with the help of gravity, would solve the problem. The project was ambitious; stacking two-by-fours to create a large storage container and then sealing all the cracks with putty to make it watertight. I never questioned or concerned myself with how the wood had materialized, assuming that if Clint was taking the lead, he must have provided the supplies. Kokia, with no other child for company, looked to us for entertainment as he sat on the ground, carefully watching our efforts. You could feel the skepticism that leaked out of his intense dark eyes, not believing, in that young body and old mind of his, that we would successfully complete anything that could truly be of benefit, especially to his mother. He was right, of course. The force of so much water inside the tank caused a considerable amount of pressure, more than the putty could hold. Our water tank never did work, and the project lost momentum.

Shortly after our garden failed, Hakim returned. He had been gone from our lives for months when Kathy threw him out, keeping their daughter, Daisy, with her in Eugene. Kathy lived on welfare in a little house that Hakim ultimately purchased for her with money from his family. I didn't object to Hakim's presence; my bonds of caring had broken, stretched so far they came back and smacked me in the face. No, I was done with this man, or at least numb to him. Now he was just another person, less invested by me with stature or influence than when we were a couple. Resisting his return didn't occur to me, nor was there a forum in which we discussed or voted on the issue. Hak just appeared. Of course he would. He was a member of our tribe. We were his home, and whether Hak moved back or not wasn't up to me. What I could do, was look forward. And I did, accompanied, however, by some ghosts of our past that kept popping up in my emotional peripheral vision.

*Hakim's cabin, Floras Creek*

Hak and I had shared a life, one with sweet times, great adventures, big hurts, and a commitment to the future. Now we didn't. Both realities existed. Who was this man and what was he to me: friend or foe, intimate or stranger, bigger than life or smaller than I imagined? On a daily basis my functional reality was that I no longer cared, at least consciously. Time, however, brought home the lesson that his leaving left more damage than could be seen from the external wound. Right now I needed to survive, emotionally and physically. If there was anything I knew, it was how to quiet my internal voice, avoiding discomfort through action. Living in a group made it easier. I wasn't alone. Every night I had company for dinner, loved ones for whom I could cook, and great support for all my endeavors. Also helpful was the fact that Hakim chose to move downhill from the main cabin, orienting toward Steve Ledbetter's and the settlement that was forming on the lower acres. Our paths did not often cross.

Along with Hak and Steve, a new couple joined us down by the creek. Kent and his girlfriend Fran had attached themselves to our group, pitching a tent in a small clearing near Steve's cabin and the water. Kent was young, sweet tempered, and well educated, his John Lennon glasses giving him away. Fran had a presence I could easily overlook. Projecting forward to middle age I could see her behind the reference desk at a library, earnest, fresh, helpful, and nondescript. But her external affect was misleading. She was more adventurous than she appeared. They were a close little sub-group down there by the creek. So close that ultimately Fran left Kent for Steve and they all continued to live as a group.

Initially Hakim's presence brought little change. New people arrived. Old friends moved on. Time meant flux. Hak easily slipped back into the familiar daily rhythms of our live-and-let-live life. He did, however, need a dope patch.

We may not have mastered a communal vegetable garden, but dope was another matter, the crop of priority for the men in our group, who once again threw their brawn into clearing plots in the forest, individually. The most critical step in growing marijuana was location; an out-of-the-way spot, difficult to access, yet available to sun. Clint was nervous about police air surveillance, particularly regarding plants on Carol's land. To put his mind at ease he rented a plane for a flyover, some of us having more access to cash than others. Sure enough, Hakim's plot down in the bottom forty was in plain view, full of ripening marijuana plants set out in neat regular rows. Clint brought the news to us at supper. Hak replanted. No one wanted to risk a bust or suffer a shortage of supply during the long, wet winter, or, for that matter, the short, sunny summer. As in any economy, priorities were set and ingenuity and industriousness paid off with results. Clear purpose and hard work yielded tall, healthy plants with heavy buds and a powerful buzz. Those who needed never went without, at least as far as dope was concerned, especially if the plots were personally nurtured.

# CHAPTER 22　You've Got a Friend

THE ROAD TO TOWN CUT THROUGH THE FARM of our neighbor, Woody, a seemingly ubiquitous name in this neck of the woods. To the north was his orchard, including several acres of apple trees, leafy and green in summer, brown and sculpted in winter, filagreed moss clinging to the bark. When we passed the orchard on our way to somewhere else, it was just another collection of fruit trees, part of the rural landscape, bigger than most but no more remarkable than streets lights in a city. Then we were invited to pick. Woody had more apples than he could use and generously offered us the opportunity to harvest whatever we wanted. Carol and I took him up on the offer, climbing into the branches on rickety wooden ladders. I staked out a tree and went higher than I liked, carrying a bucket to hold my harvest. "This apple looks almost black," I called out. "Have you ever seen one like this before?"

My reference for apples was limited to Red Delicious for eating and maybe something greener-skinned and unnamed for cooking. Until now, apples were just apples and peaches were just peaches; variety, sugar content, and lineage were never discussed, let alone displayed in grocery stores. If it was red, it was a Red Delicious, at least in name if not flavor. High up in Woody's orchard, I plucked a globe from the bough above me and took my first bite of an apple fresh from the tree. My teeth pushed into the hard, crispy flesh, crushing the tiny interior cells. Crack, a chunk of firm white meat separated from the whole. Shifting the bite to the side of my mouth I crunched down, releasing juice that bathed my tongue. Sweet or tart, the usual descriptors of apples, were inadequate for the experience. What I tasted was the essence of living soil and fresh rainwater—roots tapping the earth, leaves harvesting the sun,—the psychedelic experience of apple without the drugs. I was Alice in Wonderland. "Eat me," and I entered an alternate universe.

"Carol, take a bite. My apples are great!"

"So are mine," she yelled back, her voice slightly muffled by the leaves of the tree in which her head had disappeared.

Now I needed to taste them all. Looking around from my perch on the ladder, I spied another tree that beckoned with what seemed an even better variety. Like Eve, we always wanted more. That is the delight of fruit picking—not stripping the branches, but searching for the holy grail of produce perfection: the biggest, fattest, bluest berries, nestled so close that handfuls can be harvested in one grasp, or that golden red, gently fuzzed peach, heavy on the branch, promising juice that will run down your arm when you bite into its sun-warmed meat. Here it was apples. Yielding to the siren call of the next, I moved my ladder and reached out again, this time for a large globe, green with red striations covering its shoulders. As I chomped on the fruit of this tree I spied its neighbor hanging like a holiday decoration, pinkish red with a hint of yellow. Time to move my ladder again. On and on it went, more varieties than I knew existed, nameless but imprinted on my taste buds and memory. Beneficent Oregon was so very, very good to us.

Woody's house was across the road from the orchard. He lived with his wife in a well maintained but well used, ranch-style house that anchored a cluster of farm buildings. Behind the house were a corral and chutes for sheep shearing, some fenced land, and acres of open pasture than ran up and over the hills. On them grazed a few head of meandering cattle, a small herd of sheep, and a wild pony with her colt. Like many farms, the entrance to Woody's house was through the kitchen. In the center of the room was a round, heavily varnished wood table and three captain's chairs, lower and squatter than the ones in my parent's dining room. A practical white stove and refrigerator attested to years of use and an emphasis on utility. Sitting on the table, in pride of place, was an ever-present box of Wheat Thins, ready for a quick snack or maybe an offer of hospitality in case someone stopped by. That someone was frequently us. We were very sociable, and with no phones up the hill, communication took place face to face.

Something was always happening at Woody's. Dropping by might yield an opportunity to help shear the sheep or slaughter a steer or a peek at Woody's nudie magazine collection, stored in a discarded refrigerator in his cluttered garage, where we also skinned and butchered that steer. Woody was no fool. He had a sense of drama himself and we were audience as well as entertainment for him. Providing his own food, including killing it, was a way of life for Woody, not a novelty, as it was for us. He may have had only a few cattle grazing on his hills, but they were definitely not pets. Inviting us to help shoot a steer in the head, behead it, cut off its hooves, and then hang the carcass from a steel hook, winched over a

*Butchering sheep at Woody's, Floras Creek*

galvanized tub in his garage, was professor as showman. As carnivores we knew we had the obligation to participate in the death as well as the barbeque of our beef. Woody's offer was a challenge, a thrill, and an instructive lesson. I went because I wasn't going to be left behind, but after the chickens at Greenleaf, I knew my best shots were from a distance and with a camera.

There was, however, more to Woody's than adventure; there was also the Ritual. Arriving at his house, a group of us would disengage from the communal vehicle that was running that day. Woody would come out and exchange pleasantries, and his wife would invite us in to say hello. There in the kitchen was where the unspoken face-off—better known as "who gets the Wheat Thins?"—began. We were always hungry and that lone box of Wheat Thins sitting right in the center of the table, already open, its wrinkled wax lining folded in on itself, looked mighty inviting. Carol, Clint, Stuart, Rocky, and I, along with whoever had joined us in the truck, would stand around making small talk. Our attention was not focused, however, on the words coming out of our mouths, but on what we hoped to put in our mouths. That golden yellow Nabisco box began to glow as the spiritual nexus of the room, and clearly when you are hungry your spiritual functioning is not on its highest plane. The delicious mix of sweet, wheat, and salt were conjured up until they were almost as real as the experience itself. I could taste the crackers, could feel the sharp edges of the little squares on my tongue, the tang of the salt as it dissolved, mixing in with the crunchy pieces that broke in my mouth into smaller and smaller fragments. And I knew that my fellow communards were salivating over their own identical fantasy. The conversation may have continued, "Yup, it looks like it'll be a warm summer," and "You planted any tomatoes yet?", but the real dialogue was within ourselves.

Woody and his wife knew from past experience that if they offered the crackers, we would empty the box, leaving its wax paper innards crumpled and spent. They were done being generous. The Wheat Thins were theirs. Nevertheless, those of us from up the mountain hoped, with an intention that was laser-like in its focus, that this might be the time when they would once again offer us a little hospitality. Woody and his wife, in an act of self-preservation, assiduously avoided looking at the crackers or making any mention of sitting down and staying awhile. We knew it was fair, but our longing lingered.

To befriend us had its downside. There were so many of us and our needs were overwhelming. Once you opened the door, like locusts, we would strip the field clean. We lived in a *mi casa es su casa* world; why not just extend the boundaries a bit? With no running water on our place, keeping clean was a challenge. Steam baths were wonderful, but they were not an everyday affair. "Hey, stop by and visit when you come to town," an unsuspecting new friend would offer. Sure enough we would appear, with a freshly made loaf of bread or just our good will and joyous spirits. After hanging around and chatting, perhaps sharing a joint or two, inevitably the question would arise, "Hey, mind if I use your shower?" "Yeah, me too. I haven't bathed in days." What was a hip host supposed to do? The boundary was crossed and there we were, a little cleaner than when we started, but a little less liked. We gave, though, as good as we got. The unspoken trade was always our exotic lifestyle. We brought adventure, drugs, and the tantalizing aroma of projected sexual fantasies, functioning as dream catchers for those on the other side. We had crossed the line and there was a bit of vicarious thrill for neighbors and friends to join us for a peek.

*Milking goats, Floras Creek*

# CHAPTER 23   Strawberry Fields Forever

WE MAY NOT HAVE BEEN SELF-SUFFICIENT, except for dope, but we were hopeful. Faith paid off because food did appear through government largesse, gleaning, trading, and foraging. There were also three goats that we milked regularly, letting the milk sour and then hanging it up to drain. Within a few days, with no further intervention on our part, we had fresh cheese, artisanal ahead of our time; you just had to make sure you got there right at the unveiling or you risked sharing in the afterglow rather than the actual cheese. But like most things, our efforts were somewhat haphazard. Animal husbandry required consistent organization and intent. The little fencing we did put up was inadequate to contain our goats. Every species was left to do its own thing, a fine idea until your thing is not my thing.

We had made a group trip to town both for supplies and the entertainment of a collective outing, returning in the early evening in time to think about dinner. Katrina held Kokia's hand and carried a bag of groceries in the crook of her other arm as she approached the cabin, tired from the day and the hike up our road. The rest of us followed, balancing bags and boxes, ready to unload them in the cabin and settle in for the night. As we crested the hill and came out on the clearing, something was wrong. The door at end of the cabin was wide open, dangling on its hinges. Our eyes caught the dark rectangle of space, the entrance, which now appeared somewhat foreboding against the grey weathered boards that sealed our home. We never locked anything, there was no way and no need, but we did close our doors. Katrina got to the cabin first, but her distress reached us all at the same time. We hurried to help. One glance made it clear; we had been invaded. While we were gone the goats had wandered in and ingested everything in sight, including Clint's cooling loaves of bread. As thanks, they dropped clusters of hard round pellets all over our wood plank floor. Upstairs the chickens roosted in the loft, laying claim to space that was still home for Katrina, Paul, and Kokia. Katrina, mindful of her turf and her housekeeping, shooed them outside, and we all cleaned up the mess. The goat invasion was a lesson. Unable to fence our livestock in due to cost, will, and philosophy, we did get better at locking them out.

Our goats were untamed and our knowledge of them limited. We were given a gift of a male with the warning that they could have a strong musky smell. His odor was not the problem; instead it was his self-appointed role as the Billy Goat Gruff of our community. He would lower his head and butt us when we passed by his territory, the top of an overturned wooden row boat that was slowly recycling itself back to the elements on a pile of other refuse between the cabin and the woods. Our billy was king of the mountain and wanted you to know it. Watching him frolic, full of good goat spirits, truly kicking up his heels, was inspiring; you just had to keep your distance.

Among the guests that came and went one spring were two young men, Jeff and Hank. Their stay was brief, but long enough to have some mail sent to our box in town. Jeff was excited. He had just received a letter forwarded to him from a previous address. Stuart had picked up the letter at the post office handing it to Jeff on his way to the main cabin. The letter was written on a blue aerogram, specially designed for international correspondence when the weight of cargo on a plane really counted. Jeff was thrilled. "My old buddy. I haven't heard from him for years. He lives in Africa." He carefully unsealed the aerogram, cautiously preserving the text and return address as he unfolded the single sheet, holding it in one hand as he moved toward the overturned hull, seeking a place to sit and enjoy his letter. Our goat was nowhere in sight. Jeff climbed up on the boat, and still standing, started to read, catching up on news from his long-lost friend. Unknowingly he had just crowned himself king of the hill, a beacon and a challenge to our testosterone-charged, otherwise useless billy. This provocation could not go unanswered. Our goat rallied. From out of nowhere he came running and sprang with a leaping bounce onto the upturned boat. Should he go for the intruder or the tantalizing blue slip gently fluttering in the breeze? In one lightning move he grabbed the paper hanging out of Jeff's hands and with that bite it was gone, only a few shreds left, the news from Africa devoured in an instant. Ultimately we gave up our goats, the billy first and then the females. They were just too much work.

A vegetarian diet was cheaper and easier to provide but we did need protein, especially with such an active lifestyle. While we still had chickens, their sparse and hidden outlay of eggs was quite prized. But who got the eggs? The early birds, of course. I headed down to the main cabin earlier than usual one day. Everything was quiet except for a little smoke that could be seen coming from the chimney, probably Paul and Katrina setting their day in motion. Actually there was someone else awake and about. Sitting in a frayed aluminum beach chair, legs stretched out in front of him, was Stuart, luxuriating in the cool grey morning. One booted foot was crossed over the other and his head, covered in a wool cap, tipped back, his face relaxed and at peace pointed upwards toward the sky, eyes closed, contented. Stuart's hands were crossed over his belly and I recognized the look. Like the wolf in the *Three Little Pigs*, Stuart had used his wits, awakened first, and outsmarted everyone. He had gotten the eggs. They rested warm and tasty inside his stomach. You could feel his satisfaction. In the distance I could see Clint approaching the cabin. Soon he had crossed the central cleared space and entered inside. I joined him and we both puttered about, adding to the fire and poking around to see what we could find for breakfast. It was pretty clear that the choice was going be oatmeal with or without raisins. Nothing was said but it was felt. Today, chalk one up for Stuart, but just like the piggies, tomorrow was another day and, well, who knew just how Clint might adjust his morning schedule.

Katrina, Paul, and Kokia appeared, almost prancing with anticipation and pride. Paul led the way, triumphantly bearing the prize on his shoulder, his deep eyes glowing, reflecting the big smile beaming from his darkly bearded face. They had been to town, shopping. Together they spent precious cash on gas to make the thirty miles into Bandon and back, and then hiked up our hill laden with their newly acquired bounty. Getting everything to the cabin was going to take several trips, but on this the first run, all three were working hard, each carrying as much as they could handle. Katrina had both arms wrapped around a bag and an eye on Kokia. He in turn carried his own contribution, a plastic wrapped package of lemons, a necessary ingredient in any Greek dish. But pride of place was reserved for Paul, the paterfamilias, head of this little family. He entered the cabin with the cry of a conquering hero.

"*Karpoozi*" rang out into the afternoon and lit the switch under all of us. *Karpoozi*, Greek for watermelon and shorthand for indulgence, was a treat. Anything we bought beyond the basics was precious. Poverty, even when self-imposed, could render the most mundane item into a jewel.

*Kokia pumping water in the main cabin, Floras Creek*

The smooth green globe hefted on Paul's slight shoulder sat balanced like an oversized gem, the focus of all our eyes. Paul dropped the watermelon on the table and cracked it open. We devoured the red meat, juice dripping on the table and down our faces. Seeds spattered the floor. No worry. Later we could sweep them through the cracks between the boards. Now we were rejoicing in the moment: the rustic simplicity of our cabin, the forest around us, the precious summer sun, each other, and the grand good fortune of a watermelon. *Karpoozi*. Life was that easy.

Many nights, however, the pickings were slim. One winter evening we gathered at dusk, hopeful about dinner. I scanned for supplies. Oatmeal, brown rice, barley, and wheat berries. We always had lots of grains. Pintos, adzukis, garbanzos and white beans. Not again! Everything we had was out in the open, there being no refrigerator. A few carrots and a tomato lay to the side of the inverted wooden bowls, drying by our "sink." Then something caught my eye. A small pail sat on the shelf to the left of the woodstove. Onion skins, congealed oatmeal, some lemon rinds, and a few broken egg shells formed a mound, all destined for the compost pile, whenever one of us remembered to take it out. Sitting on top of this collection of garbage was a chicken carcass, left over from dinner the night before, picked clean, the rib cage arching above the scraps like the vaulted nave of a cathedral. I had an epiphany. Soup! Boil every last scrap of flesh off those bones, add some of the lemon rinds hiding deeper in the pile, an egg, a few odd spices, and from nothing came something: Katrina's Greek Lemon Soup a la Floras Creek. Warm up some doorstop density bread Clint had made the day before, toss a salad of scavenged wild greens, and dinner was served. Who needed a job? We could live on nothing.

By the time we ate, it was dark. A few kerosene lanterns illuminated our faces, everything outside our circle of light falling back into soft, comforting darkness. We were at the heart of the center, the core of the middle. The main cabin, surrounded by meadows, mountains, firs, and ferns, was the navel of our universe. Our own cabins, scattered throughout the woods, were the stars in heaven, beacons and anchors for us all. We were one.

Other nights were more raucous. After an infusion of cash from a stray tax return, we splurged and had steak, a T-bone for each of us, everyone in good sprits, beef our new upper. Katrina reached over to Kokia's plate and cut his meat into small pieces before starting on her own. She fussed

over Kokia, making sure he got served before the large hands and appetites around him took more than their share. Kokia finished and picked up
the real prize, his bone, meat still clinging to its spine. He began chewing,
searching the corners with his teeth and tongue, hoping to get those last
few pieces of flavor that were hard to reach. Kokia took a break. Eating
the meat had made him thirsty and he wanted something to drink. He
put down the T-shaped bone and inclined his body and attention toward
the other end of the table where there was a pitcher of water. In that moment, time extended and the noise and chatter of the table receded. Alone
on his plate sat Kokia's greasy, sparkling delicacy, temporarily abandoned
but still sporting enough morsels to make it appealing to a meat-starved
diner. Maybe he was done, maybe not. It was hard to tell. But there it
rested, as beguiling as the Sirens in a sea of want, a diamond in a field of
miner's lettuce. Carol heard the call. Without thinking she reached over
and grabbed the bone. By the time Kokia noticed, Carol was enthusiastically gnawing away, just another happy diner at our noisy table.

"Hey, that's my bone!" Kokia called out. "You took my bone!" His small
head was barely level with the big shoulders surrounding him. We all
stopped. Carol looked up, the bone in her mouth, held steady by both her
hands. Kokia was aghast. Every bit of meat was gone. Nothing was left
but a hint of flavor, Carol's slurping and sucking merely resuscitating the
memory. Kokia crumpled against his mother. The table was quiet. What
could we say? We were all hungry and the deed had been done. Tonight
was a time for good cheer. We passed around the jug of homemade wine,
reaching over Kokia's five-year-old head as he leaned his little body into
the warm side of Katrina.

We all had great appetites after physically active and demanding days. Clint
always served himself a solid portion without any fanfare. Paul, a sensualist,
appreciated each color and flavor. Stuart, brooding and a bit wry, waited for
the hubbub to die down and then took his share. Carol and I, overflowing
with words and banter, kept things moving. Sometimes Hakim or Steve
came up from their settlement by the creek to join us for dinner. The first
time Hak appeared, I felt like I was experiencing an optical illusion.

The evening was warm and we had planned some music. Steve brought
his fiddle and Hak brought a guitar, as he was trying to learn the blues.
Stuart lugged a large, slightly warped bass, almost as tall as he was, that

*Stuart in the main cabin, Floras Creek*

served more as an accessory than a musical accompaniment since he did not know how to play. First came dinner. Katrina, Carol, and I put fish soup, wild greens, and brown rice on the table. We all sat down, filling the benches, Hakim opposite me and one over. Chatter began as we shared our days. I leaned back and watched, the sound of conversation slipping into the background. Hakim sat across from me, talking and laughing, surrounded by old friends, all of us very comfortable. I couldn't help but remember that Hak and I had sat like this before, first at our small, painted drop-leaf table in New Haven, then at the long plank table at Greenleaf, and later at the same table at Floras Creek. On this night everything was the same but different. We were strangers who knew each other better than we knew anyone else in the room. Mentally I jumped between realities, having a hard time grasping which one, if any, was true.

There was one thing, however, about Hakim that had definitely changed upon his return. He was shorter. How did that happen? The answer was surprising in its simplicity: I no longer loved him. He was just another guy. When we were together, he had seemed taller, or at least height had disappeared as a reckoning point. Now Hak was back to being five feet two, no more, no less, the same height he had been when we met, the same height he had always been. I, however, had changed. It was time to move on, time for me to grow.

After dinner Paul and Hakim sat in the light of a single lantern and focused on a game of chess. The rest of us settled in for an evening of relaxed banter. Every cell in my body was at peace, nothing to prove, just internal harmony. The great Om of existence enjoined. We were and that was enough.

Then Stuart, some internal voice fed by too much wine, muttered something irritated and incomprehensible. The mood shifted. Deep in private thought, he rose abruptly and without acknowledging anyone, headed for the door, out into the dark. Nothing was said but there was a rent in the mood, which slowly resealed itself as conversations continued and Katrina readied Kokia for bed. Upstairs in the loft their soft voices, rustling in Greek, could be heard as she settled him in for sleep, a reminder that it was time for the rest of us to think about bed as well. One by one we drifted off, walking by the light of the moon to our own nests scattered under the forest of our trees.

# CHAPTER 24   He Ain't Heavy, He's My Brother

WE HAD OUR CORE GROUP, BUT STRANGERS found us and stayed, some for a few days, others longer, each with their own story. Isaac appeared like the burning bush to Moses, out of nowhere. Tall, lean, in his fifties, with scraggly grey hair and a beard to match, his eyes were intense and his manner a bit like a serpent in our Eden. His Eve was April, a young wanderer half his age. They arrived in an old school bus, which made it to the top of our hill and then to a clearing not far from mine. Once there, the bus became a permanent fixture, our own trailer park of one. Isaac was a psychologist, or so he told us, with a private practice in Berkeley that he abandoned for his new life. He was full of good tales, up for adventure, and looking for sex, or at least additional sex. Like a wolf, you could feel the predator in him. Isaac never pushed hard, but I was like a lamb being cut from the flock, one of many he sized up and approached. I could feel him panting down my neck.

On a spring afternoon as I moved slowly through the woods, my eyes down, scanning for kindling, the trees opened and I entered a small clearing between my cabin and the school bus. There stood Isaac, long legged, naked, and covered in shaggy hair from head to toe like a graying satyr. He had been watching me. I greeted him, a little startled, and the conversation moved to his inevitable topic, saving me from myself by sleeping with him.

"Margaret, you live like a nun here. Why waste your life? You're young."

"It's my business," I said, standing up a bit straighter, becoming aware that we were alone out there and my cabin was a little farther than I preferred.

"Sex is natural, a part of life. What you're doing is unnatural," he reasoned, never begging, just pressing.

"I'm not interested," I parried, trying to make a wall but foolishly not realizing that by politely participating I was, in his eyes, still leaving him opportunities.

"How do you know you don't want to sleep with me? You haven't even tried." He moved a little bit closer, his penis swinging with the step, and lowered his voice into the range of earnestness. "I'm surprised. I didn't expect you to be so closed-minded. I thought you were smart enough to leave that narrow thinking behind."

"Isaac, you're with April." I felt myself on the defensive, slipping.

"Margaret," he said and paused. "We are all with each other. What are you afraid of?"

It was an age-old line, a timeless story, except in the free-form sexuality of the present, the logic nagged a bit, but not enough. I was still trying to make sense of the fact that I was no longer married. In reality, being alone with just a cat to share my bed was about all I could handle. Isaac's desire to try the wares and make the conquest had no more appeal than similar advances had at parties when I was an undergraduate. He just felt a little more professional and hungry, fed by the hope that every commune must espouse some sort of free love; after all, why had he left his old life if not for this?

We could go for days without seeing Isaac and April, and then they would appear, bringing their talents to our pool. April knew herbs. She collected plants and hung them to dry, bouquets of tansy hanging in a row down the center of their bus. Isaac's talent was storytelling. One winter night he and April appeared after dinner, hefting burlap sacks bulging with freshly caught fish. I was alone with just the light from one lantern, getting ready to go up to my cabin. Everyone else had gone home to bed—Paul, Katrina, and Kokia having moved to their own cabin, which Paul had finally begun, if not finished.

Isaac and April had gotten a deal on several hundred pounds of red snapper in Port Orford, a great windfall. We had to gut and clean the fish that night to get them to a neighbor's freezer by morning. April lit another kerosene lantern, dimly illuminating our work area, and we carefully covered the big table with cardboard and paper. Isaac emptied out the snapper, forming a mound of fresh, slippery dead fish, gleaming in the soft light and smelling of the ocean. Each of us got a knife and started in. We sliced open the soft underside and then, bare-fisted, reached in and grabbed the entrails, looping them around our fingers as we pulled. The innards—dark, purple, and wet—were put to one side, forming their own growing mass, the light from the lanterns reflected off their glistening casings. All around us, inside and out, it was black. We could just make out, at the periphery of our light, the silvery stack of fish waiting for us, eyes open and mouths agape, and next to them the growing pile of their evis-

*Isaac*

cerated brethren. Included in the circle of light was the maroon mound of discarded offal and our own flickering faces. We were alone, just the three of us, working in the heart of darkness, feeling like the last humans on the planet. There were hours of work in front of us.

"I once had a client who was a policeman," said Isaac. "He lived murders day in and day out." Isaac paused to pick up a fresh fish and lay it down in front of him, carefully looking first at April and then making eye contact with me.

"He was called to every grisly crime scene where there were decapitations and mutilations. He would tell me about what he saw."

Something was starting to feel clammy and it wasn't just the snapper.

"Once he was called to a crime scene where the woman was sliced open from her neck to her pussy, just like these fish." Isaac's knife went in, the blade efficiently severing the soft silver underbelly.

The evening had taken a turn. What started out as teamwork, maybe not quite cozy, but at least a united effort, was curling around the edges with a sense of menace. Outside was quiet, but it seemed like a dark and stormy night. I felt very alone, my coordinates gone. Scrambling about for mental footing, my brain started to fire, seeking clues as to whether I should hightail it out of there while I could. "Who is this guy? Is he lying? Was he ever really a psychologist?" Then I admonished myself not to panic. After all, wasn't Isaac just telling stories? Apprehensive about overreacting, I stayed, making sure, however, that my alignment to the door provided easy access, just in case it was necessary. Isaac moved on to other tales and we finished the task, but the evening stayed with me, remaining part of the aura that clung to Isaac until he and April disappeared, just as they came, out of nowhere, into nowhere, leaving a strong sense of their presence and just a slight whiff of something, perhaps it was sulfur, hanging in the air.

Kit appeared one warm day, about two and a half years into our adventure, a friend of a friend of another friend, a hitchhiker destined to become a freeloader. His lineage was unclear but his presence was not. Tall, in khakis that were short around the ankle, he was definitely a white boy, his blond hair rumpled and disheveled, his sport shirt half in and half out of his pants. Kit didn't seem like a "hippie," he just looked out of it, more dazed than anything, quiet and into himself. Perhaps he had taken one too many tabs. It was hard to tell. But he, like any other member of our species, was welcome. We just gave him wide, but polite, berth.

Summer was coming and with it a big feast to celebrate the end of rain and the start of blissful weather. We had purchased red snapper fresh from the fishing boats in Port Orford at twenty-five cents per pound. Katrina, an excellent cook, was in charge of making *kakavia*, Green fisherman's soup, boiling it in a galvanized tub over our outdoor fire pit, the same tub and fire pit we used to wash our dirty clothes when a trip to the Laundromat was out of the question. Carol and Georgia cavorted around wearing turn-of-the-century sunbonnets I had found at a secondhand store. They kept Katrina company as she stirred and tasted the broth, bringing it as close as she could to the memory of the dish she had made at home in Greece. I photographed everything, wanting to hold onto the good spirits of the day. Additional cooking was going on inside the cabin, but the *kakavia* was the centerpiece of our meal, a delectable to be savored and anticipated.

By early evening the soup was done. Working in tandem, Paul, Hak, and Steve cautiously carried the tub over the cleared stubble to the cabin. They hefted it up onto the center of our long table. Our main dish cooled a bit as all of us gathered round, waiting for Katrina to clean Kokia up to her exacting standards, commune or not. Kit, moving somewhat distractedly with everyone else, was offered a spot on one of the two benches that bordered our table. There was room for us all: two rows of friends, some new, some familiar, all of us sitting shoulder to shoulder ready to dine. Hakim said a few words about being together and sharing such bounty and then the smaller more portable dishes were passed around. The *kakavia*, in its large makeshift cauldron, dominated the center, too big to move. Katrina got up to look for a small pot to use as a ladle.

While she scavenged around, Kit used the extra space to negotiate a standing spot on the bench and then he stepped up onto the table. No one said a word. Perhaps he was planning on making a toast or getting ready to thank us for our hospitality. Next Kit reached down and took off his shoes, frayed white sneakers that were already unlaced and loose on his feet, part of his inmate-from-a-mental-institution sense of personal style. Perhaps Kit was not getting ready to bless the meal and invoke the gods. Then he reached down again and swiftly rolled his pant legs up a few turns. You could feel the rumble start in our collective psyche, still unspoken, not sure this was heading in a constructive direction. And then Kit did it. Right foot first, left foot then, he was in the pot of soup, stomping and howling incoherently at the top of his lungs, head thrown back, no longer the reticent recluse but a mad desecrater of our dinner and good will. Even for us a line had been crossed. I sat looking up at him, my eyes level with the cuffs on his pants; bits of fish stuck to his hairy legs. While I watched, Clint and Stu acted, lifting Kit off the table and out the door, soup dripping off his feet as he continued to mumble and shout. Outside, just as suddenly as he had turned, Kit became subdued. Steve fetched Kit's shoes and he was escorted down the road and off the property, too much even for our all-encompassing standards.

Months later rumors floated back to us. Kit, bereft over the loss of his girlfriend, had found his way back home to Indiana. There, at his parent's house, he took acid and stabbed his mother and father to death. We never knew for sure, but it seemed plausible. Perhaps love was not all we needed; a little prudence was starting to seem necessary.

*Laundry, Floras Creek*

# CHAPTER 25 You Can't Always Get What You Want

OUR ONLY STRUCTURE WAS NO STRUCTURE. We chafed under charts and rules. Actually, we never got that far. We chafed at the idea of charts and rules. Dishes could sit for days in the wood basin by our hand pump. One by one we plucked them from the pile and washed them on an as-needed basis, either for a lone snack or a communal meal. After we ate they were returned, freshly smeared and crusted, to the dry sink from whence they came. We trusted the universe to provide, another way of saying we waited it out to see who gave in first. In the morning it was just as easy to pick a dirty bowl out of the pile, scrub it individually, eat your oatmeal, and then carefully place it right back in the stack. "I'll get to it later" was our functional mantra. "Hey, I did my part, I cleaned everything two days ago" was our silent justification. It wasn't until Katrina and Paul moved into the main cabin that housekeeping occurred with any regularity or met any consistent hygienic standards. Katrina was a gift from god, myself a lesser acolyte. We needed help.

It was time for some agreements, written or not. Even tribes have laws, often unforgiving ones. We had to start somewhere. Carol, an only child, had grown up with maids on the upper east side of Manhattan. Her parents, Mike and Minnie, worked long hours in the family health food store, leaving at around 9:00 in the morning, returning after 8:00 at night. Carol's grandmother cared for her until Carol was old enough to be left alone. Daily lessons on working together to share the family load were not the stuff on which Carol was weaned, unless it was being viewed on Ozzie and Harriet. To top it off, pragmatics were not always Carol's strength. Being brilliant, funny, irreverent, and ready for adventure was much of her charm, but it did not always translate well when work was needed.

On the commune, as elsewhere, I got things done; you could depend on me. Dinner needed to be cooked? I jumped right in. Someone to heat and haul water, I was right there. The main cabin a mess, I was all over it, along with Katrina, my partner in non-crime, two straight arrows let loose. Clearly we were carrying the heaviest loads, at least among the women, who at that point were down to three regulars and some revolving guests. I was frustrated. Carol was fun, but that wasn't enough. We needed help. Katrina and I were cleaning a stack of dishes from breakfast,

YOU CAN'T ALWAYS GET WHAT YOU WANT    175

a necessary preparation for dinner, when I stopped, greasy bowl in hand, and confronted the reality.

"Katrina, you and I are doing all the work."

She looked up from nursing a flame in the stove's firebox. "I know, Margaret, but what can we do?"

"Carol needs to help out more. We need to talk with her."

I was pretty pleased with my idea. We could talk it out and arrive at a solution. After all, we were rational beings, committed to community and peaceful means of problem solving. Wasn't that what the mantra "make love not war" and all the dope smoking were about? My thinking sat on principles. It also rested, just as firmly, on my fear of confrontation. I may have been mad at Carol, but I certainly wasn't going to show it. Who knew what I might say if I got angry. Maybe something ugly and upsetting would spew out, unleashing the raw sewage of hurt and resentment. I didn't want to get blasted by the force of my own naked feelings, and I certainly didn't want to be on the receiving end of Carol's either. Her retorts could blow me to pieces or sweep me into the emotional swamp of mea culpa where I would berate myself for not having done better, for not waiting until I could craft the perfect phrase that would nail the issue on the head and bring home world peace. No, I was not going to shoot straight from my emotional hip. I chose the Age of Aquarius, the more transcendent, loving solution that would leave me smelling like a rose, at least to myself.

We sat down to talk on a sunny day, cool and comfortable under the branches of an old gnarled tree. Below the canopy of leaves I could see the dry, yellow grasses of late August. Carol leaned against the trunk and Katrina and I sat cross-legged, the three of us forming a small circle, Kokia our satellite off to the side hunting bugs. The day was lazy and quiet, insects humming in the background. But this was not a time to relax; we had business. I took the lead.

"Carol, we need more help from you in the main cabin," I said, carefully maintaining a reasonable non-accusatory tone of voice. "Everyone is in and out and no one ever really cleans up after themselves. It feels like Katrina and I are carrying too much of the load."

First step accomplished; the topic is now on the table and we are ready to move on to a civilized, emotionally contained conversation.

"Sure, I'd like to help. What do you need from me?"

Was she kidding? The list was endless, but I slid past that thought and soldiered on. "The guys get up early, make breakfast, and then go off to cut wood, leaving their bowls and cups scattered on the table and their dirty pots piled in the sink. It's hard to get mad at them because they do so much, but I am tired of always doing the dishes."

"So don't do them!" One thing about Carol, she did not get hung up on niceties.

To me it was heresy. Don't do them? How could I not do them? I quickly bashed that thought down. Like the mole-in-a-hole carnival game, my job was to obliterate its provocative presence. Not be responsible? Then who would I be? I took a quick mental survey and tried another tack. "You're right, I could leave the mess, but we all share the space and we all need the bowls and pans for dinner."

"Let them clean up after themselves. I didn't come here to be anyone's housewife." She had a point, but I knew it was just that. My tack was not working. Frustrated, I finally hit the confrontation button.

"Well, you try changing things! You figure out how to get everyone to keep the place clean!" This was language Carol understood.

"Okay, I get it. But really Margaret, it's hard to help. You get everything done before I even get a chance to do anything. Zip, zip, you have it all cleaned up and by the time I think about it, it's too late. You're so speedy there is never anything to do."

Whoops, things seem to have shifted here. How did this happen? Now it's my character that is being scrutinized and found lacking. She's right though. I am a go-getter, a bit of a Goody Two-Shoes. Well, I certainly don't want to be found lacking. I am happy to fix that and right away.

"You're right, Carol. I do take charge awfully fast. How's this? What if I try to support you by slowing down? That would help because everything wouldn't be done before you noticed and got moving on it."

Satisfied, I breathed a sigh of relief. I was quite pleased and happy to ignore the tiny question mark that was beginning to form just at the horizon of my consciousness.

"I'm glad we worked this out." I said as we relaxed into the afternoon.

But of course we hadn't. The conversation was ridiculous. What made me think that through talking change could occur? I was giving peace a chance, but was peace giving me a chance? How do people actually get along and work toward a common goal? I didn't know, but I doggedly kept trying.

# CHAPTER 26 | I Am Woman

CAROL AND I, OR AT LEAST I, CONTINUED TO STRUGGLE with our personal differences. Where we easily came together was as women, particularly as there were so few of us. During the off-season, the harshness of our existence winnowed our female population to three: Carol, Katrina, and me. We needed each other. Summer was the exception, with friends and strangers arriving to enjoy the novelty and pleasure of our lifestyle. As fall of our first year in Floras Creek approached, guests moved on; Georgia headed east for her medical studies and Sharon, her friend, returned to Texas. During her few months with us Georgia had been an enthusiastic participant, fitting in comfortably with our community, so comfortably that she and Clint developed an intimacy that grew past the bonds of friendship. Carol's wariness, the day Stuart left us all on the beach, was justified. Georgia and Clint were now a couple. Carol wasn't Lisa or Janet. She was a solid, middle-class Jewish girl who had no interest in sharing. Clint was her hunky, handsome, goyisha hero—solid, steady, and firmly rooted enough to resist her push. Carol had abandoned her career, moving west to follow Clint, ultimately buying land that fulfilled his dreams more than hers. The times may have changed, but oh how we strong women, no matter how hard we tried, continually got ensnared in the age-old act of yielding, the line between our thrill of being in thrall and our undoing a very thin one. Now Clint wanted another woman. Carol was enraged and devastated. She was not going to share her man, and she certainly wasn't going to sit around and watch while some other woman got what she treasured. Shocked and hurt, no longer at home on her own land, Carol fled to Footbridge, our sister group. Within a few weeks Carol discovered she was pregnant, letting Clint know he was about to become a father through a postcard with a line drawing of a pregnant woman with "Guess Who" scrawled across the top. With this news and the change of seasons, Georgia headed off to medical school and Clint left for Footbridge, ready to bring Carol home where they could settle into parenthood.

During the winter it was easy to feel isolated, hemmed in by short days and incessant rain. We had left the larger world and now felt the smallness of our own. Without media we were isolated from the events of the day.

While we debated the fate of chickens, struggled to understand community, and learned to live with less, the rest of the world carried on: Black September at the Olympics, the Paris Peace Treaty, Nixon's resignation, and girls admitted to Little League. Huge parts of the culture were lost to us as we worked to build our own world. Bits and pieces wafted through but they seemed distant. One particular incident, however, stands out as cutting through the haze.

Carol and I heard rumors about a new magazine called *Ms.* Published exclusively by and for women, *Ms.* offered, instead of handy household hints and husband pleasing suggestions, articles with titles like "Money for Housework" and "Body Hair, the Last Frontier." Within a year of its inception, *Ms.* published an in-your-face petition to decriminalize abortion. It was signed by fifty-three prominent women who performed an act of civil disobedience by telling their stories of terminated pregnancies. Other articles informed us how to write our own marriage contract, de-sex the English language, and raise children without gender roles. As difficult as it is to imagine now, this was revolutionary, a big run in the silk stocking curtain.

"Right on," Carol and I told each other, but how to get a copy? Our local magazine supply was dominated by hunting periodicals and girlie rags, limp with well-thumbed pages that curled over the edges of the display rack by the cash register. This called for a trip to the library. Carol and I pooled our money for gas and drove down the mountain, turning north at the coast highway for the additional thirty-five miles to Coos Bay. I parked my old truck and we started inside, an aggressive presence from the moment we crossed the threshold of the quiet, carpeted room. We, who grew up in libraries, the cathedrals of our upwardly mobile world, were now brash, bold, dirty aliens in their muted rooms. But we didn't care. We were mountain women and proud of it. With the curly hair of our ethnic background flying free, Carol and I stepped forward, ready to claim our magazine.

"Do you have a copy of *Ms.*?" we politely asked the librarian who womaned the desk in her print dress and stockings, Carol and I oblivious to any bonds of sisterhood outside our own world.

"Yes," she replied pleasantly and pointed to the correct shelf. We located the issue and carried it off to a corner where we could devour it uninter-

rupted, thrilled with our discovery. The times, they were a-changin'. *Ms.*
was our voice, unapologetic and above ground, not a crudely printed hippie rag but a slick publication, ready to be seen and taken seriously. Carol
and I took turns holding the magazine, reading over each other's shoulders. Mission accomplished we headed home, smug and happy, where
our choice of nineteenth-century technology kept us more fettered and
submissive to men than we had ever been, even if we did know how to
chop wood.

Being a modern woman in the woods was confusing. I burst with power when I hefted my axe, felt its weight, and brought the blade home,
chopping wood to fire my own stove. Yes, this was me, Margaret, a strong
woman, without a partner, satisfied and happy. But what did it mean to be
strong? Male skills were the gold standard. I honed mine as best I could,
but I knew I was dependent on Clint, Stuart, and the rest of the men to
survive. This was bitter fruit, as the feminism of the times proclaimed us
equals; women were as hard and tough as men, we just needed to claim
the territory. Softness was out. In an effort to break the shackles of gender,
we were exhorted by our sisters to throw the baby out with the bath water,
to devalue the nurturing inwardness of womanhood and embrace the very
traits of our oppressors, classic Frantz Fanon. Our efforts could not have
been any more self-annihilating. If we had to hurl ourselves into manhood
then so be it. Radical change called for radical measures. I signed on the
dotted line and threw myself into the task, trucks, tools, and toughness at
the ready, proud of my ability to change.

In reality, my challenge as a single, childless woman in the woods was
nothing compared to the Sisyphean task that Carol and Katrina faced
daily: bearing and caring for children under primitive conditions. Adding
insult to injury, being mothers meant being marginalized. After all, what
could they do of value? Care for children? That's nice but what about helping the communal good? Sure, sure, sure, children are great, but what can
you *do*? As young adults we were indulging ourselves, the restrictions of
parenthood beyond our ken. We were the kids.

Katrina felt it the most. She was tiny, had a young son and later the addition of a new baby. Her husband's greatest strength was as a contempla-
tive, a dreamer. Paul could be here now, as Ram Das exhorted, in the moment, immersed, one with a leaf, the sky, or a game of chess, even when

not stoned. The challenge lay in moving from the present to the future, which is how things get done, through action. Paul moved slowly, if at all. He wasn't lazy. Paul just got waylaid in the wonder of the moment, often leaving Katrina with the practical realities of daily life. Katrina, small in stature and fully responsible for Kokia, lacked the strength and time to take on big physical chores. Even more than the rest of us women, Katrina was dependent on others for assistance.

"Can't we set up a plan, some way we can organize the work?" she suggested at dinner. "I'm good at cooking and keeping the main cabin clean. Those are tasks I can do and still care for Kokia, but I need some help with other things, like firewood for the stove. Maybe we could set up a schedule for different men to provide wood for the main cabin."

What was she thinking? Didn't she know who she was talking to? A plan? How long had she been here? Katrina's reasonable request, this and others, evoked one of two responses. The first was no response at all, the conversation catching for a glottal stop, a brief pause, her words thrown out and then lost as chatter resumed, almost uninterrupted in its flow. Did someone speak? Maybe, but not anyone we really have to listen to, power being its own reward. If this were not insulting enough, the alternative was more brutally direct, even though it was couched in the laid back, trust to the universe rhetoric of the times.

"If you want to cook, go ahead and cook. If there's no wood, then don't. It'll all work out. Someone will get wood. Dinner will get made."

Katrina was coming to realize that she could not survive. Paul was supportive, but not supportive enough, and far too slow, even when their intentions were aligned. Carol, on the other hand, had Clint, our most effective provider, who could ease the challenge of pregnancy and motherhood without amenities, though even he could not eradicate them.

I was happy to have Carol back and often went to drop in on their cozy home. On one visit, while Clint chopped firewood outside, Carol and I sat crossed-legged, close to the stove. She had just received a package from her Aunt Susy in Manhattan, a blue and white layette set from Saks Fifth Avenue, artfully displayed in a creamy ivory box, tucked under sheer sheets of delicate tissue paper, each piece folded and arranged like two dimensional origami, awaiting a tiny newborn body.

"How cute," I cooed.

*Clint and Cheryl's cabin, Floras Creek*

"Saks," said Carol, pointing to the box and pulling a knowing face, happy about the baby, her Aunt Susy's sense of taste, and of course the ridiculousness of such finery against our torn clothes, dirty boots, and grimy fingernails. Clint came in with a load of fresh wood in his arms and put it near the stove to dry, setting himself down near Carol, his hand briefly on her belly.

"What does it feel like for you," I asked him, interested in a father's point of view.

Clint thought for a moment while Carol made a wisecrack. "What's for him to feel? Just look at this belly, I'm doing all the work here." Clint took being Carol's straight man in stride.

"At first I didn't like the idea of having a baby," he mused. "I felt trapped. Then this other part of me started asking, when am I going to have a normal relationship with a kid and commitments? Am I just going to fart around for the rest of my life?"

"Normal?" Carol snorted.

"It's nice not having those kinds of responsibilities—a  mortgage, a steady job, financial pressure."

Just listening to Clint, I started to wilt. His litany seemed so oppressive.

"It took a bit of thinking. The bachelor started dying and the husband started to awaken. You know that a guy is attracted by anything that walks by, anything that will offer . . ."

"Men," Carol interjected knowingly, rolling her eyes in my direction.

"Yes, Carol, men." Clint's voice was firm. "Every young man grows up like this. It's like that movie we saw the other night where the poor guy's working in a gas station but sees himself as a race car driver." They were able to watch a movie in the comfort of their rustic cabin because Clint had rigged up a system using car batteries to run a small television, an olive branch to appease Carol's sense of isolation from media and her career.

"Then all of a sudden he's got a kid and a temperamental wife and he has to work every day. Remember when the guy got a chance to go fishing with his friend and get back to being something other than just a grind. There's still a little bit of that left in every guy. Things start closing in and you want to hang onto all that footloose and fancy-free stuff."

"You mean you don't want our baby?" Carol's sass was melting under this onslaught.

"No, no, that's not it at all," Clint protested. "Everything is rewarding in its own way, some are kind of shallow and others have a deeper, more long-lasting reward. It's just hard to give up the boy and become the man."

"What about Georgia?" Carol was ready to pick at old wounds.

"You and I were together, but we weren't tied," Clint explained. "I didn't see anything like the affair with Georgia as permanent, just more food on the table, so to speak, more variety. It wasn't like you and I were married. Yes, we had a commitment and a dog, but when we decided to have a kid that changed everything."

I got up. It was time to put another log on the fire.

Katrina went into labor first, her daughter Lena born late February of 1973. Like most winter nights, it was windy and rainy and Katrina, with that nesting instinct of late pregnancy, wanted to get everything in order. Kokia needed a bath before bed. She brought in the big galvanized washtub and filled it with hot water that she had hand pumped and heated, pot by pot, on the stove. Toward the end of the bath Katrina felt a small pain, her discomfort gradually becoming more pronounced until it was clear she was having contractions. When they started to come with regularity Katrina knew it was time to drive down the mountain to the small clinic in North Bend.

Paul bundled himself up, grabbed a flashlight, and walked out the door to find transportation, as they had none of their own. Later Paul told us about the night. Cold, wind-driven rain was beating down, soaking his face and snaking up his sleeves, gusting at him from shifting directions. Paul headed for Clint's cabin, a quarter-mile away and a sure bet for a running vehicle. When he arrived, Clint and Carol were nestled in for the night but quickly got up, ready to help. Clint drove to the main cabin and dropped Carol off to care for Kokia, taking Paul and Katrina with him, bumping in low gear all the way to the bottom of our hill, where Carol's car was parked. Hunched against the weather, Paul and Katrina climbed out of the cab and into the front seat of Carol's car, water gushing in rivulets, sheeting across the unpaved surface of the logging road. Driving under these conditions was dangerous. Clay slime from the run-off formed a slick on the roads. If the car got stuck in a ditch there was no way to get it out, just a long hike back up our path or ten miles down the road to

*Paul, Kokia, and Lena at Floras Creek*

the main highway, empty at this time of night. Paul turned the key in the ignition, grateful that the car started immediately, not necessarily a given in our world. Peering through the rain, he gently eased out onto the road, trying to be sensitive to Katrina and hoping to avoid getting stuck in the mud. Glancing at the dashboard, he realized that the gas tank was dangerously low. There was nothing to do but give it a try, coasting as much as possible on the downhill stretches.

Halfway down the mountain the road became paved, but Paul continued to drive slowly, about ten miles an hour, while wind-whipped rain, pelting against the windshield, made it hard to see. Leaning forward, straining to pick out where the road began and the underbrush disappeared, Paul's eye caught the form of something in the weak beam of the headlights. A lone buck was standing, still and alert, at the edge of the woods, dark against the wet and murky forest, its antlers an echo of the surrounding tree branches. The buck turned its head and took note of the car and its inhabitants, a small but deliberate awareness, and then bounded in front of them, close enough for Paul to see its hooves disappear into the hillside. He took it as a good omen, an avatar in the night.

Paul and Katrina made it to the country clinic, no bigger than a house, with a tiny waiting lobby and one nurse on duty. It was 3 a.m. Paul inquired after the doctor and was assured that he would be called when the time came. The nurse whisked Katrina away into the delivery area and left Paul with a set of surgical scrubs to slip over his clothes. He was grimy from the rain and mud and hadn't taken a bath for days. Before Paul could even finish tying the strings at the back of his sanitary smock, he had smeared it, leaving wet brown stains on the cuffs and hem.

Lena was born at eight in the morning on a brilliant sunny day. She spent her first hours nestled next to her mother on fresh white sheets, with an indoor toilet and hot running water just a few steps away. Katrina relaxed into being clean and cared for, reluctant even after three days to return back up the hill.

Two months later, after a long labor and a cesarean section, Carol gave birth to her son Huckleberry at the fully equipped hospital in Coos Bay. Like Katrina she returned home to rustic circumstances: a woodstove that required feeding almost as often as the new baby and water for drinking and washing that was hand pumped in the main cabin and lugged home in plastic jugs. All the wounds, cuts, tears, and lacerations of childbirth were theirs to tend, just not with ease. No heat packs were available to loosen an engorged milk duct, soaking baths to sooth delicate tissues, or daily showers to keep clean and fresh as the womb shed its lining. The commonplace realities of recovering from childbirth, complicated in Carol's case by surgery, were suffered without these civilized aids.

Just as Carol and Katrina's bodies rearranged themselves, organs shifting back into place and size, hormones recalibrating from pregnancy to nursing, so did their identities. For Katrina, a second-time mom, it was easier, but a new baby calls out for care and her protective instincts left her feeling vulnerable. Carol, who was still trying to resolve the conflict between her career and her man, was catapulted into an alternate reality where independence was a fading vision. Together Katrina and Carol were our mothers, celebrated and rejoiced for the new lives they had brought, part of us but a group unto themselves, marginalized together as they cared for their babies.

When Lena and Hucky were still infants, a few of us went to the beach to gather mussels, an opportunity for adventure and entertainment even with the wind and fog that settled at the coast. While everyone spent a few hours scavenging for dinner, Carol and Katrina remained in the cab of the truck. At first it was fun for them, nursing and chatting. Bit by bit time slowed. Frustrated, Carol turned to Katrina and put it all on the line. "How come we're stuck in the truck, while everybody else is having a good time?" Of course they couldn't leave the shelter of the cab. They were women with babies. It was windy and misty out there, too raw for an infant.

Katrina knew it was time to return to Greece with or without Paul. Kokia was old enough for school and Katrina needed better circumstances for herself and her children.

"I hate the fact that we're asking for something for nothing when we get food stamps," she told me as we scavenged through supplies, looking for scraps to cook for dinner. "I never set out to beat the system. I was, and still am, quite a middle-of-the-road person." Katrina started to cut up some bruised tomatoes for soup. "We're not better than everyone because we're different. We think we're great because we function outside social borders. The truth is we're not."

I listened, wide-eyed. This was one step from blasphemy, but hitting close to home.

"There is a lot of talent going astray here," Katrina said as she rummaged through the dirty dishes, looking for a pot for the soup.

I said nothing and continued to slice up zucchini.

A few months later Katrina left with the children while Paul stayed at Floras Creek, none of us clear whether this was a final or temporary split. What was obvious was that Paul, who was enjoying his newfound bachelor status, was in no hurry to return to Greece. I missed Katrina and felt badly she had to leave, clearly knowing that her choice was the right one but saddened that our community was not enough. Later she sent a letter that surprised me. After returning home and luxuriating in cleanliness Katrina had a revelation.

"I think living in Floras Creek changed me," she wrote. "Believe it or not, with all my complaints and feelings of not belonging, once I left, I felt I had gained a great experience, a real sense of belonging. I have good feelings about the place and about everyone there. Clint was such a pillar. He emanated confidence. That was important to me because I felt very insecure. You and Carol were the highlights. Carol was very entertaining, she made things interesting, and you made things warm. Now that I am back I feel different. I look around and view so much of what I see with a lot of contempt."

I missed her very much.

# CHAPTER 27   This Land is Your Land

THE QUESTION OF LAND OWNERSHIP peeked sporadically above the horizon of our awareness, waving a little flag, calling out, "Look at me! Look at me!" We averted our eyes and avoided the issue until it gained a foothold and demanded our attention. Clint and Carol had been visiting her parents in Hallendale, Florida, introducing them to their young grandson, when the rumblings began. By the time they returned, an ambush was in place.

There had been little discussion of land ownership prior to our present high noon. When we left Greenleaf, almost three years before, there were two givens. Carol was purchasing land and we were staying together. The motivation for buying half a mountain seemed so obvious there was no need to ask why. Hadn't we kissed our careers good-bye for the woods? Of course we were moving with her. Did you leave your children or spouse behind when you relocated? Clint and Carol may have talked behind closed doors, but I never heard a whisper of doubt.

We all knew that Mike and Minnie, Carol's parents, had put up the money for the land. I took this as a stroke of great good luck. Thank you, Carol. Thank you, Minnie. And now let's pick up where we left off, but this time on a permanent basis. Nothing led me to believe differently. Even after the incident with Don and Mary Ellen, the significance of ownership took a few years to ripen and release seeds of doubt among us. Is it ours? Is it theirs? Do we pay? Can we stay? Rumors of a conflict between Steve and Clint floated in the air.

Floras Creek had two sections, the upper 120 acres purchased outright by Minnie in Carol's name and the lower forty, where the creek flowed, mortgaged jointly by Carol and her mother. Shorty sold them the water rights on the lower piece, but withheld the timber rights, holding out for more money. Steve Ledbetter, using a small inheritance from the death of his mother, negotiated with Shorty and purchased the sought-after timber rights. His intent was to support a communal holding, Steve's way to make a contribution and move the ethos away from a single owner and back to the group. Steve also paid many of the monthly payments for the lower forty, taking responsibility for himself and those of us who had no funds.

Steve traveled back East for a few months the winter of our second year. Before leaving, he gave Clint cash to cover the payments in his absence. On his return Steve noted that $1,000 beyond the monthly costs was missing. Where had that money gone? The discrepancy became a big topic of whispered discussions, fed by outraged sensibilities. No clear answer came to the fore. There were some mutterings about discretionary spending on the part of Clint. I was incensed. What right did Clint have to take the money and use it for himself? This was our land. Ultimately, Clint gave Steve an old green jeep. It may have evened out the financial debt, but it left Steve feeling psychically burned. Lines were being drawn. Ownership needed to become clear. The lower forty was the plum, water and trees trumping acreage. Carol and Minnie understood value. They wanted it all. Some private negotiations took place. Minnie bought out Steve's timber rights and reimbursed him for the mortgage payments. Now everything was clean: no confusion, no doubts, no loose ends. A picture was coming into focus, but it was the wrong one. A single headshot was emerging where we had anticipated a group portrait. Accumulated discontent rose to the surface. Hakim, always attuned to his constituency, corralled the scattered conversations into one big debate and drove it in the direction of confrontation. A meeting was called.

Hak and his delegation—Steve, Fran, and Kent—arrived en masse from the creek with Hak settling himself strategically in the middle of the bench that flanked the outer side of our table. Paul and I joined them in the main cabin. Stu, always one step to the side, arrived by himself and a little late, situating himself more as an observer than a participant. Rocky, full of ingratiating energy, found his spot down from Hakim. We awaited the arrival of Clint and Carol, who had recently returned from their two-month visit with Carol's parents. I was anxious and self-conscious when they appeared in the doorway, Carol holding Hucky in her arms.

"Hi. Got any pizza? We were hoping for the delivery boy," Rocky nervously greeted them, attempting humor in an effort to diffuse their discomfort as well as his. The delivery of a severed horse's head would have better matched the mood. Carol followed Clint around the table, scooting in after him. They settled to my right facing Hakim, the sides drawn, our own Yalta, our personal Paris Peace Accord. It was time for the negotiations to begin. Carol opened the discussion.

"I know everyone's been talking. So have Clint and I. A lot has happened while we were gone. You know I always wanted my own land." Nursing Hucky, she shifted him to the other breast, his dark brown eyes calmly surveying the scene as he suckled away. "I like everyone here. My mother put up the money. I . . . I . . . Clint?" Carol looked over at Clint and without saying anything made it clear that she, whose medium was words, wanted him to continue and to speak for them both.

Clint, steady and even, his big frame anchoring his family, picked up where Carol left off. "This has taken us by surprise. We know that every-one wants some partnership in owning the land."

Hakim listened, alert; the face-off was now between him and Clint.

"Carol and I got back from Florida to find that everything has changed."

Here was Hakim's cue. He pounced, but very deliberately, his voice low but loaded.

"Nothing has changed. We all came here for a new life, a better way of living." He started easy and built up in intensity, hitting his rhetori-cal stride, confronting Clint and Carol while simultaneously rallying the troops.

"This is our land, for all of us, together. Where is our future if it belongs to you? Our labor, our effort, our dreams are here; here where we are building our homes, here, which is our home." Hakim pounded on the ta-ble with his index finger marking *here* for all of us to see and feel. He was a community organizer, an activist in his own neighborhood now. "We have left behind old ways of thinking. Why would you keep us divided into rich and poor? A tribe shares its land. Greed pits us against each other."

Nursing babies, friendships, financial realities, nothing mattered; no, he had a point to argue, all eyes were on him, his mouth pulled tight as he faced off with the land owners. Hak was an unwavering, formidable force, with theory on his side and determination fueling the ride. Carol and Clint felt the pressure; the decision regarding ownership ultimately rested with them—thumbs up, thumbs down, it was all theirs. They sat alone, backs up against the wall.

The financial dealings that led us to this point had barely registered in the pragmatics of my daily life. It was irrelevant to me. Living in the Prom-ised Land, in a state of trust, I had no money to share and felt secure in the love of my friends. My world did not feel threatened. I was too integral a part of the whole. *L'état, c'est moi.* Clint had taught me how to lay out my foundation. Carol had supported my pluck, glad that I didn't wither under the loss of Hakim and abandon her by fleeing to the city. The thought of financial consequences or the need for recompense never entered my mind.

Paul was more realistic. Katrina, fed up, had returned to Greece with the children. He knew, with the draft no longer a threat, that at some point he would follow, but for the present he was in Floras Creek and land ownership was the topic of the day. Fran, Kent, Steve, Rocky, and Hakim had met in Paul's cabin to hold one of the many discussions that had taken place in Clint and Carol's absence. As Paul listened to Hak's diatribe against Carol, he was confused by the space between the words and the underlying realities. Later he told me, "Hak's never going to live here forever. He's a man of the world, a city guy with lots of ambition and family money. This isn't his ultimate future." Paul was also surprised by the bitterness and animosity toward Carol. How did it get to be class confrontation, us against the man, with Carol as the establishment, her friends and fellow communards now attacking her as selfish, hoping for her demise? Paul understood that Steve and Fran had fewer prospects in front of them and thus more to lose, but where was Hak's drive coming from except intellectual prowess combined with political dogmatism. To Paul there were other solutions. If we were all so committed to having land together, we could find another piece nearby and join forces, not so different from how we already lived with some of us down by the creek and the rest by the cabin. But Paul kept these thoughts to himself. He, like everyone else, did not want to openly challenge Hakim's stance. Besides, his real focus and attention were elsewhere. In the face of Katrina's absence and possible permanent separation, Paul was effectively single and enjoying it. Greece was home, but now was not the time to do much worrying.

Rocky had no illusions. Experience taught him the world was not offering much, especially for free, but he was always happily grateful for what did fall his way. As he had many times before, Rocky was ready to pack his bags and accept that he needed to move on. Luck had been with him so far. How could he complain, especially having no money to contribute? But Hakim was persuasive and Rocky did like living at Floras Creek, so he joined the battle, but not with a committed heart.

Clint was caught in the middle. His dream had been rugged, undeveloped wilderness, not a domesticated farm. To please him, Carol bought

Floras Creek. But Clint and Carol had not moved alone. The hills were dotted with shacks that anchored a dozen lives. Clint wanted to live as part of a community. Carol was ambivalent, torn between her desire for a rustic love nest and the camaraderie of the group. She was, however, clear on ownership. Floras Creek was hers, an investment in property. This was a problem. Carol bought Clint the land he wanted for an unexpectedly high price, her independence. Now she had property but she was dependent on Clint for survival and on us for company. The woods could be a lonely place, especially for a fast-talking, urbane entertainer. Clint felt the competing pulls as he tried to walk the line. From time to time he lost his balance and wavered. Then he righted himself and found his center. He was Carol's partner. This was a long-term investment.

Each piece fell into place, adding momentum. Carol felt blindsided on her return from Florida, under attack on her own land, with not even Clint fully in her camp. She knew that Hakim had framed the confrontation, ideological on his part, but that did not make things any less lonely. Stuart, who was not vested one way or the other, was somewhat of an ally, along with Paul and his more pragmatic approach. Carol was mad at me for siding with Hak, and she made it known, sitting on the steps outside my cabin, Hucky in her arms.

"I am clear on this, Margaret. There is no question in my mind as to where I stand and how I feel about anyone who sides against me. I like you, but I no longer feel safe in your presence. As for Fran and Steve, I never had much in common with them anyway and now I dislike them intensely. This is where it stops. There is a point where I have to protect myself. I am not giving up ownership of my land." She took a minute to unbutton her sweater and let Hucky latch onto her nipple.

One breast out, the green, green trees of Oregon all around us, Carol picked up without missing a beat.

"You have resources, Margaret. Everyone here has money, or property, or something. This is mine. What are you going to bring to the table?"

I sat beside her, listening, but that last point hit home. Maybe just being me wasn't enough; trading myself and my goodwill was coming up short against cold hard cash.

Carol continued, relentless. "Your parents are twenty years younger than my mother and father. Why don't they help you buy your own land? Paul's family has land and olive orchards in Greece. Hak's family has money. What if I asked Paul, 'Hey, Paul, would you give me part of one of your vineyards?' or Hak, 'What about ten acres in Bali and I will trade you something for it?' Come on Margaret, get real. This is just a little too far into Weatherman country for me. I feel taken advantage of. There is no way I can survive here without everyone, but this is an investment. This is my inheritance and I am not giving it away." It was hard to get much clearer than that.

I was torn. Carol was my closest friend, but where was my future? Without these people on this land, I was bereft. My parents were not going to give me any money. Earning a living in the woods was nigh impossible. There was no way I could save and purchase my own property, which I didn't want anyhow. I liked my new life with everyone. Now it was being threatened. We had each hit our bottom lines, fighting for investments that were defined in opposing terms. I too was up against the wall.

"Why do you want Floras Creek all for yourself? What about what we're trying to build here? Don't tell me you want to live in these woods with no one but Clint." I got up and walked around, kicking at the chips by my chopping block. "I don't get it. What do you want, for us to be your renters? No one is asking to get something for nothing. You heard everyone. We'll all contribute. What are our choices?"

My arguments were more questions than solutions, more emotional than pragmatic. I still held onto hope, feeling Carol's need for mutually exclusive realities. Carol could get stuck, repeatedly vacillating at the apex of a decision, preventing resolution in one direction or the other. Now we, as well as she, were all victims of her conflicting desires, which, in fact, had been in play from the beginning. East coast, West coast. Actress, writer. Clint, no Clint. Career, hippie. Ownership, community. These conflicts had informed Carol's actions from the time of her original reluctance to leave New York and follow Clint out to Oregon. She wavered on all of them before getting accidentally pregnant and committing, at least for the time being, to Clint, motherhood, and the land, which at that time came with a community of communards. Now the final issue had to be addressed, money, and on that Carol knew her bottom line. "The land is mine, Margaret. I own it."

Carol knew the costs, the value, and the purchasing history of Floras Creek. I, however, was unaware of who owned what and how many acres were at stake or that there were even timber rights that were sold separately. With great emotion and little fact, I aligned with the Good and joined the loose alliance Hakim built to make a stand for communal ownership. There was no way I could afford to look at it from any other point of view. I was a believer. My new faith was based on raw need. Love one another, be good, and don't bother yourself about practicalities. I had become one with the hippie creed. Ironically, I was Hakim's best student. Carol's very practical sense of ownership did not resonate with me. I was still a child in the world of adult finances.

Hucky fussed and she moved him to her other breast, giving both of us a chance to shift our focus for a minute. With him settled, she bent over and pulled back his diaper to check on how fresh it was.

"How were you ever married to him?" she asked, looking up from her son's bottom, her voice softer, quizzical. I knew just what she was saying. Carol had finally felt the steel in Hakim. "How did you do it? There is no way to argue that man down. He doesn't care what anyone else wants. If you get in his way he'll run you off the road." I nodded my head in agreement, pleased to hear my feelings validated out in the open, comfortable back in our role as friends trying to understand the men in our lives.

"Jesus fucking Christ." Carol's attention was turned inward, reliving the fight in her mind. "He almost makes me doubt myself. When he goes on and on, arguing each point relentlessly, he wins in a way. Hak forces me to see the other side and then I feel guilty and wrong. But you know what?"

My face lit up. "What?"

"Too fucking bad!"

Obviously Carol was no patsy herself, even if she had let Clint do the talking for her. "Maybe I'm selfish and not behaving in an idealistic manner, but when Hak goes back to Indonesia and Paul returns to Greece who is going to be here, responsible, taking care of things?"

I listened, relieved to know that the feelings of moral failure I experienced under Hakim's expert tutelage were not unique to me, a glimmering realization dawning that I had been worked, and by a pro. Worst of all, that pro had been my husband.

While I shared Carol's frustration with Hak, I still shared Hak's vision. If there was any chance that we were going to own the land collectively, I knew I would have to find a way to contribute my share. Clearly my cooking and charming company would no longer be considered an adequate exchange. I needed to support myself and pay my way as, in spite of Carol's stance, I still assumed that some form of joint ownership would work. The red flags in this, my second marriage, were wildly waving in the wind but once again I seemed unable to register their import. I gave no thought to the fact that property had value and represented the investment of hard-earned monies in a world where you earned your capital and respected its worth. Hadn't Hak thrown our cash on the table? Didn't we all share? Faith seemed enough at the time. It wasn't. Nothing was resolved around the table that day, but there was no escaping the hard reality of money. We thought we were far out. We weren't. Our ranks were infiltrated and the enemy was us. We were our own Trojan horse, ownership deeply embedded in our DNA. We couldn't see it, but the future was written.

# CHAPTER 28 Can't Buy Me Love

I NEEDED MONEY. Some locals told us about brush picking. There was a shed in Langlois where the owners bought ferns and branches of Oregon grape harvested from the surrounding forests. From this collection point, the greens were bundled and trucked down to cities farther south to be used by florists in bouquets. The plants were free for the picking. You just had to drive into the woods, snip and stash, fill the bed of the truck with nature's bounty, and bring it home at the end of the day to exchange for another kind of green. I could do that. It beat trying to waitress. Stuart and I set out in his truck. The drive through back roads and into the woods was lovely.

"Where are we going?" I asked, always needing coordinates in life.

"I don't know. We'll drive 'til we don't."

"This look good to you?"

"Yup. Looks like woods."

We parked, grabbed our burlap sacks from the back of the truck, and walked, scanning for leaves that resembled those at the shed. My biggest fear was getting lost. I could not stray too far from Stuart. He was my ticket back to the truck.

Even though the woods were beautiful and the hours flexible, it didn't take long for the job's drawbacks to become evident. The plants were easy to spot, but pickers before us had cleared the roadside, forcing us deep into the forest. As we spread over the landscape, Stuart was not always close enough or in the mood to be chatty. After an hour of admiring the beauty surrounding me, my mind wandered. Looking for leaves had its limitations, boredom being the main one, the second being that it was not a particularly lucrative profession. If it were, the woods would have been crawling with pickers just like me. In reality it took a lot of walking, looking, cutting, and heaving to fill the truck, and one truck's worth did not fill my pocketbook. I could see this was a full-time job. If I wanted nine-to-five employment I could have stayed in town and earned more.

I wracked my brain for ways to bring in money. Tucked away, carried from the city to the farm to the mountains, were a few precious items from my past life: an iridescent beaded purse from the 1920s, my netsukes, and an antique silver hand mirror. Odd that in the beauty of our rustic life I still treasured these delicately wrought artifacts. Even Kokia, whose first conscious spiritual experience was of walks in the Oregon woods with his father, was drawn to the baubles of civilization.

Kokia had only a few toys—one dented rusty Tonka truck and three faded matchbox cars. The stores in Bandon and Coos Bay were full of fresh, brightly painted novelties—toys, trinkets, and treats. For Kokia they were perfect and pristine, enticingly displayed in row upon row of eye level shelves. These bits of the "normal" world, a place where a glistening piece of candy or an enamel red racer were everyday items, sent him into giddy fits of hidden delight and covetousness. Secretly he would reach out, taking sweets and little toys, pocketing them, overcome by his desire for something more.

Kokia knew it was wrong but he also knew, even at his young age, that there were different kinds of rule breaking, varying hierarchies that could be used to adjudicate self worth. About an hour away from us was small commune, Manzanita, where another little boy, Flow, about two years younger than Kokia, lived. Laura, his mother, was unkempt and afloat in a parallel universe, more like an escapee from a mental hospital than a political activist, even though she owned the land on which their fluctuating group lived. Flow's father was unknown. Laura shared leadership with James, a sociopath with clear blue eyes who radiated a Charles Manson-like chill. They were not a couple in any traditional sense of the word. One afternoon while we were visiting, Laura ran into Hakim on the path that led through their property. Circumventing social niceties, she let Hakim know that she wanted to sleep with him. When he indicated that he was not interested, Laura, nonplussed, stuck her grimy hands into her pants and started to move her arm rhythmically up and down. She was masturbating, standing right there on the path, amazing even Hakim, who came back and told the story with disbelief.

Flow, whose name was apt for a bare-bottomed toddler, had a sad, pinched little face and a bedraggled demeanor, lacking in any of the joy that should be natural to childhood. On a visit to Floras Creek, Flow wore oversized, scuffed, hi-top brown leather shoes, minus socks, and a second-hand jacket that buttoned up the front, covering him from mid-buttock to chin, leaving him naked in between, except for smudges of dirt. We drove down to a shallow swimming hole. Flow did not want to go in. Instead, he squatted by the side of the water, digging with a stick, an urchin out of a Dickens novel. Before leaving, Flow pooped right on the beach, giving his waste, like a feral animal, a light dusting of sand. Kokia's sensibilities were offended. He too might have been shaggy, but Kokia felt sure he was a step above Flow. Maybe Kokia foraged from waste bins at the back of the store or secretly stole toys from the front counters, but at least he didn't poop on the beach. Kokia was the prince of the royal holdings . . . Floras Creek. Greek manhood asserted its indulged pride at a very early age, even on foreign turf. Flow, Kokia let his mother know, was definitely from a different caste of the communal hierarchy.

I, however, was an adult and knew what I had to do. Kokia pilfered. I needed to divest. Taking my hand-beaded purse and silver mirror to a small antique/used goods store in town, I stood at the counter in my rough and rugged clothes, hair askew, and offered up these refined and delicate little pieces of craftsmanship. They offered me twenty dollars. That meager amount was not going to get me anywhere. The real answer seemed obvious if unpleasant. I needed a job.

A hand-scrawled sign in the window of an unpainted concrete block building advertised work. A new fish store was opening on the coast in Port Orford and they needed help, a handyman to assist in getting it up and running. I had built my own cabin. Didn't that make me handy? Feeling, if not full of bravado, at least sufficiently needy, I put on a veneer of bluff, walked in, and applied for the job. An older man with a stubble of white beard and an unkempt ring of hair on his partially bald head was inside, used refrigeration cases askew in the empty cinder block interior. Clearly he was just getting organized and probably not looking for any finish work. That was reassuring, as I did have a strong sense of my limitations. I introduced myself and presented my case. To his credit, he did not turn me away but was open to having me start working right then and there, a pretty sure sign that he was in over his head as much as I was.

"The roof leaks. Find the cracks and caulk 'em up," he instructed me as we headed outside. "The ladder is out back. I'll show you the problem."

Caulking was an undeveloped skill on my part. We were used to cracks as a way of life and if a structure leaked, there was always more tar paper. "Sure," I replied, actually more worried about the ladder than my skill, as heights were somewhat of a problem for me. We climbed up together, him leading, me following, economics the driving force for us both. I needed the money and he needed cheap help. Up on the roof he showed me the caulking gun he had been using and let me know he would be inside the store if I needed him for more supplies. With that he left, to my relief, as now I had to figure out how to use the gizmo. The process was pretty straightforward—cut an angled opening on the spout, insert the tube of caulking, extrude the goo, and move slowly along the crack to form a seal. "I can do this," I thought. But I couldn't, at least not with any acceptable skill. Keeping a straight line was a challenge; the caulking came out in irregular waves, tending to resemble swag on a wedding cake, amateurishly applied at that. Using my finger I tried to even out the white goop, moving it from where there was too much to where there was not enough, a nice try, but no solution. Clearly I had bluffed myself into an impossible situation. The thought of cutting my losses and slipping out was very appealing, but I would have to pass in front of the store, with its big glass windows, to get to my truck. Having my new boss watch me sneak away in an effort to save face was more face-losing than I could handle, and I did need some money. Instead I climbed down and confessed my ignorance.

Ozzie, my boss listened with a slightly perplexed look on his face, but he didn't get mad and he didn't laugh. He seemed to accept the absurdity of the situation, as I did, front on, ignoring the degree to which success was impossible, yet hoping that it might magically make itself manifest and save the day. Together we were suspended in that state of grace, that wonderful defense mechanism, pretending something does not exist because we wished it wasn't so. "Okay. Let's go back up and I'll show you how to do it," was his reply. Patiently Ozzie demonstrated how caulking was done, keeping an even movement and a steady hand to ensure a smooth bead. I took the gun and tried to follow his lead, but like any skill, mastery takes practice, and it was becoming clear to both us that my efforts applied under our mutual gaze were unsatisfactory. Nothing needed to be said at this point but, "Thank you for giving me a try." Together we climbed down and I got in my truck and headed back up the hill, embarrassed and still broke.

That left only one alternative. A few days later I put on clean jeans, my lace-up logging boots, and my best secondhand sweater and drove back to Port Orford to apply for a job at the local bar. They hired me. With happiness and foreboding I became a waitress, thrilled at my opportunity to earn some money, mentally calculating the tips I could earn. The foreboding came from a grim acknowledgment, reality pushing delusions aside, that waitressing at a backwater bar was not much of future, especially as I still had those pesky college loans to pay off. Threatening letters had found me even though my address was a tar-paper shack. Carol suggested that I try sending loaves of homemade bread to pay down the debt, an idea that had us cackling as we imagined bricks of our hand-ground, wood-fired bread landing on the desk of some governmental flunky in Washington.

I reported for work, once again with no experience under my belt. How hard could it be to take orders and deliver them to a table? The bar was packed with fishermen coming in for a drink and a bite after a long day at sea. There was a second dining room in the back of the restaurant, away from the conviviality of the front room and bar. This, the owner indicated to me, was my station, failing to note that it was rarely occupied. When fishermen came in, they took their usual spots up front. They waved to waitresses that were like second spouses, steady, familiar, and knowledge-able about their particular appetites, there day in and day out for a lifetime of growing up and now old together in this home away from home. Not me. I was definitely not one with this tribe. They had set me up. To them I was a joke, the living incarnation of something they saw on the tele-vision above the bar or hitchhiking along their familiar roads, amusing and strange but relatively harmless, good for a few laughs. Being in that position was uncomfortable, but somehow I understood. I was, after all, trying to be different, staking out new territory that ended up making me a foreigner in my own land. I was as odd to them as they to me, each of us viewing the other with self-satisfied, condescending acceptance, tolerant except for the occasional jab here and there. That, at least, was the rela-tively benign reality at the restaurant. Elsewhere I was to learn the world could be much more hostile, reducing me to a two-dimensional hippie deserving of nothing but disdain, a lesson brought home over a pair of boots.

Your footwear defined you as clearly in the woods as it did in the city, the variation in work boots as big a statement of country machismo as flats, pumps, or stilettos were for urban womanhood. Steel-toed, crepe soles, ankle-high or lace-up—these were critical choices, telling the world what work you did and what you thought of yourself. I got it. Boots were also an investment; as my one and only pair of footwear, durability was impor-tant. My needs were clear—strong enough to protect me if an axe grazed the toe, roomy enough for several layers of socks, and waterproofed to seal out the rain. But no one said they had to be ugly. I went to the army/navy store in town and looked around. One pair caught my eyes. They were rough, black cowhide with round steel toes, thick hard soles, and stacked heels. Most importantly, they laced all the way up to my kneecap, the fashion statement I needed. No boring brown work boots with white crepe soles for me. No sireee. I needed these babies. Walking away from the store, I felt sassy. Nothing like the strut of a woman who feels she is lookin' good. I was a hot, shit-kicking momma, queen of the backwoods, with the lifestyle and clothes to prove it. Some things never change.

But very soon I noticed the sole of the right boot was starting to crack directly under the ball of my foot. It was a nasty crevice that went from side to side. Armed with the receipt, as I was a very responsible shopper, I returned to the store to ask for another pair in exchange or my money back. A salesman referred me to the manager, who was straightening a rack of canteens. I walked over, past several aisles of fatigues and field jackets, and approached him. My boots were in a bag. Clearly he would be able to see the date on the receipt, the fact that the boots were hardly used, even if they were muddy, and the severity of the crack in the sole. My innocence should be self-evident. "Hello, can you help me? I think I bought some defective boots," I said, reaching into the bag to bring out the proof. The manager was a ratty-looking man, with thin, greasy hair, rather rough around the edges, like some of his merchandise. He looked straight at me, not breaking into a gracious please-let-me-help-you smile, as I expected, but standing there impassive, making it clear that his sense of me was even less charitable than mine of him.

"What'd ja do hippie? Take a hoe to 'em?" he said. "I'm not giving you no money back. You wrecked 'em and now you come in here lyin' and tryin' to make a fool of me. You bought 'em. They're yours. That's it."

I was shocked. What happened to rules? Where were civility and fairness? Who does he think I am? I'm not a liar. My hair may be wild but my morals aren't. These boots, not me, are defective. The manager turned and disappeared up another aisle, leaving me with my bag and the disputed evidence. I'll take him to small claims court, I thought. He can't get away with this.

But he felt he could, and that was my biggest loss, much greater than the cost of the boots. I may have felt like queen of the backwoods, but the manager looked at me with the eyes of an Okie from Muskogee. People really hated me. I, who teachers loved, policemen helped, and salespeople had once fawned over, had become a reviled outcast. Grace was gone. Hostility prevailed. I had rejected the status quo. Now it rejected me with a vengeance, a hard concept for me to absorb.

Back at the restaurant I was grateful they had at least seen clear to hire me, offering me an opportunity, even if it was limited. I knew I had to start at the bottom just like everyone else, taking a few orders, absorbing a little ribbing and letting them take my measure. Fair enough. I was willing to give it a try, for a while at least.

Carrying an order to one of the few occupied tables in my section, I passed by the bar. One of the men raised his hand and signaled me over, calling out, "Hey you with the hair! How's it going?" This was followed by drunken laughter from his cronies on their stools. They knew all too well how it was going, and slowly it dawned on me as well. I was losing money, spending more on gas to drive up and down the hill than I was earning. My other loss was lifestyle. Fitting into the grid of time put me at odds with everyone else at home. With a clock to punch I found myself anxiously checking my resurrected watch to make sure I was not late to work. Sorry, I have to go, and not with the flow. I was an alien in the harmonics of my own community, a cost that I could absorb for a while, but the constant insults added to my financial injury were not the pay off I had so optimistically calculated. What could I do? Perhaps if I stuck it out I might get a better station and more respect.

Within a few shifts my truck brought reality home. Finishing work at midnight, I headed out to the parking lot, ready to face the dark ride up our mountain followed by the long hike to my cabin. Turning the key in the ignition, I stepped on the gas and heard the whirring of the starter, but not the catch of the engine. My truck was old and sometimes it took several tries to get started. Tired, but dogged, I repeated the process, concern starting to register somewhere between the fourth and fifth effort. Maybe I had flooded the engine. I sat and waited and went through the steps again, the parking lot empty as everyone had gone home. After several more tries it became official; I was stuck, no choice but to sleep in the truck and hope that as dawn broke someone might come along and help. If that didn't work, maybe someone on our land would notice I was missing and drive down to the bar. My prayer was that I wouldn't have to hitchhike up the mountain, standing by the roadside, vulnerable and tired. Resigned, I stretched out on the seat of the truck, head at the wheel, knees curled by the gear shift, and settled in for the rest of the night, knowing that my career as a waitress had come to an end.

Some hard truths needed to be faced. I had hit the unyielding limitations of poverty. Vehicles that didn't work were fine as long as you didn't have to be anywhere. Low-paying, time-consuming jobs did not compensate me financially or spiritually. Money became a critical fulcrum on which the success or failure of my efforts balanced. I was teetering precariously.

The night I stepped on my glasses I felt the shift. Every night before sleeping I lay in my loft and read by the light of my kerosene lantern. As my head started to nod, I took off my glasses and placed them on the ladder by my bed, the two by four rungs set in the wall providing a neat little shelf. That same ladder was my route to the tin can tucked in a corner under the loft, my nighttime urinal, a much more appealing solution than squatting outside, especially on cold and rainy nights.

This particular night I awoke with moonlight coming through the windows set behind my bed, barely lighting the interior of my cabin. Deep in the molasses of sleep, a warm tingly feeling formed, slowly coalescing until awareness broke through—time for a rendezvous with my makeshift plumbing. Oh, but it's so warm under these covers and so cold out there, the embers in my stove long gone. I nestled in deeper and drowsily faced the big question, do I drift back to sweet sleep and ignore the gentle pressure I am feeling or face the inevitable and just do it, get out of bed and hit the can. Quickly I threw back the covers and stepped out on the ladder, ready to make a fast run, trying to keep the warmth of my bed in my mind if not on my body. With that step all urgency shifted from my groin to my foot. Something cracked. Damn, it must be my glasses. What a fool. I found the flashlight and took a look; one arm had broken off my glasses and the other, still attached, hung askew. Luckily the lenses were still fine. My heart sank with the instantaneous awareness that I didn't have enough money to replace them. This was big trouble.

Letting go of expectations and embracing change was all fine and good as far as concepts go, but I had run out of space to yield. This was my Waterloo. I was caught in the quicksand of poverty, which can impose an enforced passivity or call for epic struggles to move beyond its grasp. As immigrants to the new world my grandparents had opted for the latter, scraping lives out of nothing except bare-knuckled willpower to create their vision of a better life. Me, I turned the dream around, throwing away everything for which they had worked, albeit for the same end, and now I was stuck. The moment of truth had arrived. My heart fell. It was time to leave and get a real job. Maybe, just maybe, if I earned enough money and got unemployment, I could return to Floras Creek, which I hoped would still be a home for me. Maybe I could even send some money back. But for now it was time to go south.

# CHAPTER 29  The Long and Winding Road

STUART, CAROL, AND I DROVE INTO BANDON to pick up some brick ends that the cheese factory in town sold at half price. On the way back we stopped to visit Lee and Lester, our biker friends, socializing and shopping on the same tank of gas. Stuart and Carol disappeared into the back of the house, looking to share a toke or two. I found Lee in the kitchen, waiting for his ride to the highway. He was leaving for a bus trip to San Francisco. On their kitchen table, along with crusted dishes from long past meals, was a handmade carpetbag that Sue had sewn from a left-over piece of rug, making magic out of nothing. Inside were a few pairs of overalls, some homemade bread, and fresh goat cheese. Next to the bag was a plastic gallon milk container, crumpled in at one corner, remnants of a washed-out label still sticking to the front. Lee had filled it with water, enough to last him for the bus ride.

"Ready for your trip?" I asked, brushing off some crumbs before I sat down.

Lee looked deflated, his usual spirits dampened. "No," he replied emphatically.

"Why not?" I queried, confused.

He hesitated, his face behind his big black beard as open as a child's. "I don't like leaving here."

"It's always hard to be away from your family," I replied, solicitous.

"No, no, no. That's not it. Of course I'll miss everyone, but it's more than that." Lee opened both his hands and looked at me, full of questions. "Here I am, a full-grown man, and I'm scared. My knees are shaky. I don't want to go out there."

He was a *paisano* leaving the village for the big city. No kindergartner setting out for his first day at school could have been more fragile. We were freaks, outsiders to the rest of the world, insiders to each other. Stepping out into the world alone, we were naked. He knew what it was to be part of a clan, close to his group and others like it. Away from the hearth of community there was nothing but chill. In any other circumstances, I wouldn't feel a kinship with Lee and Lester. We wouldn't even know each other, let alone feel a shared bond. If Lee—tough guy, biker, doper, and dropout—could be brought to his emotional knees at the thought of temporary exile, then what hope was there for me? We were nothing without each other.

Months later, when it was my turn to leave, Stuart drove me to the bus stop on the highway. Like my immigrant family before me, this time I too was traveling to the land of milk and money, planning on making some and sending a little back. The worm had turned. On a grey January day, damp and overcast, I stood with Stuart on the gravel shoulder of the coast road, his truck parked off to the side, the unmarked bus stop a holding place between two worlds. I tried to absorb everything, wanting to take the firs, the mist, the ferns, my whole world with me as I prepared to depart. One by one I placed them inside, ingesting their living freshness and all the memories they carried, knowing I was going to have to live off the sustenance of the past for a while. Waiting for the bus, I looked south down the road and felt a chill enter my core, reminding me of the vastness ahead where my coordinates were unknown and the vistas less forgiving. I was venturing out, naked, no bundled layers of intimacy to protect me. A draft was entering my life; the back door to my snug little world was hanging open. This is temporary, I mistakenly told myself, the lie I needed in order to leave. How could I go back to living isolated in an apartment, every day spent inside in an office, binding my hair, my mind, and my body into a more conventional shape when the woods, my friends, every change and adventure, were my true form? "You are either on the bus or off the bus," said Ken Kesey as he and the Merry Pranksters drove across country in their psychedelic bus Further, always their ultimate goal. Seven years ago the painted chariot of the Hog Farm pulled into my life. Today the only bus I awaited was a Greyhound.

We had tried to create our own myths. Up on our mountain we cavorted and fought, struggled and screwed, just like the gods, bound to our natures and each other. Now, after five years, it was time for me to step down, out of the Oregon mists, a Hestia for modern times. Like the goddess of the hearth, I carried the sacred flame of home and community within me.

The bus appeared. It was time. I hugged Stuart good-bye and boarded, bound for San Francisco, my own re-filled plastic water jug cradled under my arm, tight against my body, short-term sustenance, but a drop from the pool that has sustained me ever since.

*Hóka héy*. Today is a good day to die.

*Margaret at Floras Creek*

# Epilogue

WHEN I LEFT, I THOUGHT I WOULD RETURN. What I didn't realize was that we, the self-chosen people, were on the cusp of a diaspora. While I was in San Francisco, Clint and Carol made their final decision; the land was theirs, unhindered by any subcontracts or clauses. At my departure I was still hopeful that a compromise would appear. Within weeks, however, the finality of the situation became clear; there was no future in staying. No one had to tell us to leave; we did it ourselves, the realities of ownership, world politics, and personal tragedy emptying our ramshackle structures. I was now spiritually homeless, a stranger in a new city without cabin or community, returned to the future I had fled, but at a lower starting rung. The hard truth was my move was not temporary. This was now my life. Stubbornly I refused to even visit the ever-dwindling group that remained. Instead, I stayed in San Francisco writing environmental impact reports, stuck on a swivel chair under fluorescent lights while my body longed for the vibrating thwack of an ax as it split a fragrant round of cedar in the fresh air of Oregon.

Paul stopped by my apartment in San Francisco on his way to Greece. In 1974 the right-wing junta had collapsed. Now he was returning home to claim his career and family in a safe political environment without the threat of the draft. Back in the straight world, Paul's ability to sit for hours and merge with the trees became more of a liability than an asset. Still, he managed to work as an architect and support his family. Katrina moved forward, putting her organizational skills to use at the US Embassy in Athens, where she was a senior cultural affairs specialist. They both retired in 2009. Kokia and Lena, with dual citizenships, were able to attended college in the States and return home for summers on the Aegean. After graduation, Kokia settled in Oregon and now moves between Greece, Turkey, and Portland with his wife Daphne, sharing lives dedicated to kundalini yoga, health, and art. Lena returned to Athens where she lives with her husband and works as an architect. To date they have no children.

Hakim left Floras Creek sadly accompanying the body of his youngest brother Hamdan home to Indonesia. Hamdan had arrived at Floras Creek after my departure. He had come for a visit but stayed, buying a fishing boat with Kent, who lived on the lower forty. Against the advice of experienced fishermen, on their first outing they set off into a storm and capsized. Their bodies washed up several days later, Kent's lashed to the mast of their boat in a futile effort to stay alive.

Once in Indonesia, Hakim accepted his destiny and became an executive. Daisy, his daughter with Kathy, remains in Oregon. Hakim and Steve continue to be friends, visiting each other often, setting aside time for golf and business deals. Steve stayed in Oregon, where he purchased land and raised the son he had with Fran. A few years ago, Steve moved to isolated property in Northern California with his most recent partner.

Indonesia continues to play an important role in Roggie's life. After arriving in 1972 disguised as a Sikh businessman on a counterfeit ticket, he stayed for ten years, studying classical Javanese court dance and co-authoring a book on the history of Javanese culture. From dance he moved to theatre, and back across the Pacific, where he spent twenty years in Dallas and Los Angeles. Roggie is now in Texas after a volunteer stint in Jakarta and Papua with Peace Brigades International, an NGO inspired by Gandhi that uses protective accompaniment to support human rights defenders who are threatened with violence.

Guy and Janet left the commune after our move to Floras Creek, seeking spiritual enlightenment first at the Self Realization Center in Los Angeles and then at an ashram in Oregon where Guy served as the personal architect to his guru. After several years, Guy and Janet returned to Texas and followed separate paths. Guy remarried and has a private architectural practice that promotes green construction.

Don and Mary Ellen, the first casualties in our property dispute, split up. Mary Ellen stayed in Eugene and studied nursing, developing new strength and great generosity of spirit. She died of cancer ten years ago. Don married and moved to Hawaii, where he lives with his family and works as an architect. He and his wife assisted Mary Ellen as she struggled with her disease.

Six months after my departure from Floras Creek, Stuart visited me in San Francisco, seeking relief from the winter rains. He stayed. When I got pregnant, we moved to Los Angeles, into a house down the block from Clint and Carol. She was trying to restart her acting career. With the birth of our first daughter it became clear that staying home and caring for my baby was not an option. I needed to work and contribute to our finances, necessity once again my muse. I began assisting at a family day care to defray the expense of part-time childcare for our daughter. Eventually I took over the business and, with the birth of a second daughter, all four of us moved into the child-care house, the only way we could survive financially. Money was no longer simply an issue; the need for it was a fact. Stuart was unreliable. I had to work for us to survive.

My union with Stuart was precarious, but within its fragile shell our daughters were solid ground at the center of my universe. These were lives I had to protect, relationships that never ended. The family day care thrived, allowing me to be home with them as well as twelve preschool-aged children who arrived at 7:30 each morning and stayed until evening, often joining us for dinner when their parents were late. Each night before bed, my daughters tucked away their toys, preparing their bedroom for the nappers who would sleep on mats laid out on the floor the following day. The master bedroom became an art room, a space set aside for painting and creating, but not procreating. Stuart and I shared the remaining bedroom. Our living room, furnished with couches from families that had moved on up the decorating scale, was the central play space. Orange shag rugs ran from wall to wall. Gritty sand that clung to bare feet and crumpled pants settled among its twists. Everything was always dirty no matter how often I cleaned. Our bookcase had a space reserved for building blocks as well as stacked narrow shelves that were slanted for display. Instead of popular novels we had the classics—*Good Night Moon* and *Where the Wild Things Are*. This was no way to raise my family.

Stuart and I separated when our girls were three and six. On my own again, but this time with a business in place, albeit a very small one, I made the push for a real school. The effort took time, a commodity that was hard to come by for a single parent. At night I made presentations to attract investors. By day, in addition to caring for my own children as well as those of others, I fought city hall, plodding through hearings and arcane regulations, focused on moving permits forward. My degree in city planning was finally being put to use. Lessons from the woods were applied as well. I dug deep, not in the dirt, but inside, fighting for the right to use the property I had purchased and continued to hold, the first step in my next dream. Friends and clients became the community that I looked to for support as I stormed the bureaucratic barricades. Luck and tenacity were on my side. I won.

Sanctified by the zoning department and deeply in debt, I faced another obstacle, wrestling with my contractor to remodel at a pace and price that fit my limited budget. He did. After ten years of living in the family day-care home, seven of them as a single parent, I moved the preschool to its new location. This now is my utopia. Walk through our gate and the world drops away. Friendly is the operative word and love is my currency. I need this.

Once I found my pace at the preschool, I returned to graduate school, one course at a time, to get a master's degree as a marriage and family counselor. Now, in addition to my school, I have a small private practice as a family therapist. Although I settled in southern California, my daughters have completed the circle. They both live in Portland with their families, seeking much of what I sought there, but in tune with another generation; one is a vegan baker and entrepreneur, the other a visual artist and devoted mother.

Stuart became an accomplished craftsman and custom furniture-maker but was not able to match business success with his talent and skill. He got sober in 1983 and remained sober until his death in 2006, when at age sixty-eight, he passed away from complications of early Alzheimer's. Our daughters managed his care at the end of his life, sitting by his side as his mind and body slowly failed.

Clint and Carol were able to keep residences in both Oregon and Los Angeles. When Carol is in Los Angeles, we live within arguing distance of each other, as we have for forty years, raising our families, building careers, sharing mutual respect for our disparate talents while our opposing temperaments clash. After five years, Clint and Carol sold the property on Floras Creek and bought land on another mountainside in Oregon, down the road from Johnny and Tchanan, who never left their self-sufficient lifestyle. Clint and Carol's new mountain rises out of a gentle valley with orchards and fenced fields that surround their home, a ranch house complete with plumbing and electricity. They live alongside a creek that flows through arching alders and summer gardens, bordered by hedgerows of blackberries, warm and dusty in the sun.

It took me thirty years to visit.